Latino American Literature in the Classroom

Florida A&M University, Tallahassee
Florida Atlantic University, Boca Raton
Florida Gulf Coast University, Ft. Myers
Florida International University, Miami
Florida State University, Tallahassee
University of Central Florida, Orlando
University of Florida, Gainesville
University of North Florida, Jacksonville
University of South Florida, Tampa
University of West Florida, Pensacola

Latino American Literature in the Classroom

The Politics of Transformation

Delia Poey

University Press of Florida
Gainesville · Tallahassee · Tampa · Boca Raton
Pensacola · Orlando · Miami · Jacksonville · Ft. Myers

07 06 05 04 03 02 6 5 4 3 2 1

Library of Congress Cataloging-in-Publication Data
Poey, Delia.
Latino literature in the classroom: the politics of transformation / Delia Poey.
p. cm.
Includes bibliographical references and index.
ISBN: 978-1-61610-131-2 (acid free paper)
1. American literature--Hispanic American authors—Study and teaching. 2. Latin American literature—Study and teaching—United States. 3. Hispanic Americans in literature—Study and teaching. 4. Politics and literature—Latin America. 5. Politics and literature—United States. I. Title.
PS153.H56 .P64 2002
810.9'868073071—dc21 2002016570

The University Press of Florida is the scholarly publishing agency for the State University System of Florida, comprising Florida A&M University, Florida Atlantic University, Florida Gulf Coast University, Florida International University, Florida State University, University of Central Florida, University of Florida, University of North Florida, University of South Florida, and University of West Florida.

University Press of Florida
15 Northwest 15th Street
Gainesville, FL 32611–2079
http://www.upf.com

In memory of my parents, Roberto Poey and Delia Alcázar de Poey,
who taught me so much about crossing borders.

Contents

Acknowledgments

The completion of this project would not have been possible without the help and encouragement of a long list of individuals. I am particularly grateful to Leslie Bary for her help with the early conception of this project, to Carol Batker, Jerrilyn McGregory, Donna Nudd, and Stacey Wolf for reading countless drafts and offering their guidance and critique, to Anita González and Carrie Sadahl for their continuing support, to Kelly Tompkins for editorial help early on, and to Virginia Trujillo for making the manuscript readable. I am also grateful for the consideration given the manuscript by the University Press of Florida, and most especially Susan Fernandez. Most of all, I am indebted to my daughters, Alex and Gabby, who persistently keep my priorities in order, and to my husband, Virgil, whose love and support make anything possible.

Introduction

Borders are imaginary lines, drawn to invoke the effect of containment. The illusion is enforced by fences, walls, bold black lines on a map, or "natural" borders, such as water. They are constructed for purposes of inclusion as well as exclusion. They are meant to keep things and people in, as much as keep them out. To subvert the purpose of a border is an act of contamination, a violation of the principle of containment. Perhaps it is because the process of border construction has proven so successful that crossing these arbitrary lines while carrying the contraband of language, ideas, culture, or human experience from one side to the other proves so difficult. Once a border is crossed, the object becomes decontextualized. It metamorphoses into something else.

Several years ago, when the movie *Malcolm X* was released, along with its ubiquitous merchandising, teenagers in Mexico City could be seen wearing the black caps with the white X. A Malcolm X cap, outside of its U.S. context, becomes emptied of its meaning. It becomes, in more ways than one, *una gorra equis.* The phrase literally means an X cap, but it also means much more and much less than that. In Spanish, *una gorra equis* is a common cap, a cap like any other. It is undifferentiated and therefore interchangeable with any other cap. The X or *equis* carried across the border is also the algebraic unknown. *Una gorra equis* is then both a particular cap, with an unknown but specific meaning or set of meanings, as well as any cap.

It could be argued that crossing the same border in the opposite direction, from south to north, is more intensely an act of decontextualization. Given the proliferation of U.S. popular culture outside of U.S. borders, particularly through mass media, the rest of the world has a much broader, even if sometimes warped understanding of the United States, and a much more varied set of images from which to form a conceptualization of U.S. culture. The First World, in this instance specifically the United States, is constantly invading the Third World nations that share this hemisphere.[1] Of course, the cultural flux is not solely north to south. Latin America is also invading the United States, but such a flux is still disproportionate.[2] This leads to the conclusion that the United States has a much more limited vision of its neighbors than they have of it. As a result, an American object—meaning pertaining to the states, since the English language does not provide an equivalent to *estadounidense*—is less open to the processes that affect cultural images carried from south to north.

The proliferation of reproductions of Frida Kahlo's paintings in the form of posters, calendars, postcards, and book jackets illustrates this point. Kahlo's work is particularly vulnerable to decontextualization because of its self-conscious fashioning of a Mexican iconography. The appropriation of Frida Kahlo became a charged issue in 1992 when Chicana actresses protested the production of a film based on Frida Kahlo's life because its producers had planned to hire an Italian American actress for the lead. The media covered the protest, and attention shifted from issues of appropriation to those of artistic freedom (Fusco 26). Frida Kahlo, who reinvented herself as the embodiment of *mexicanidad*—even changing her birth date to coincide with the year of the Mexican Revolution—had become a fetishized object. Her life and work were deemed fascinating enough to be the subject of a Hollywood film, but they were simultaneously perceived as palatable to a mainstream audience only if the cinematic version homogenized her difference.

These examples, which highlight the processes of transformation that affect all culturally specific productions—and what production is not culturally specific?—are parallel to the processes through which a text, produced at the margins of the Western literary establishment, is subsequently brought into circulation within the academy. As David Theo Goldberg articulates: "As nations acquire borders, so disciplines acquire boundaries, and for much the same reason: for policing and self-policing what can be said and done, for ordering the unacceptable and the foreign, and for licensing membership and citizenship" (Goldberg 27).

Transformations and translations are inherent in any border crossing. Issues of "authenticity" are irrelevant in this context.[3] Because appeals to "authenticity" have been discredited as embedded in colonialist and imperialist discourses of domination, we must avoid falling prey to the use of such simplistic models and pry deeper into the processes at play, as well as examine our own role as participants in a hegemonic discursive area such as the academy.[4]

There is a broad range of possible responses to cultural productions from beyond the border. At one extreme is the practice of silencing them or rendering them invisible by simply ignoring their existence. The other extreme, appropriation and colonization, is more subtle but no less troublesome. Negotiating the space between these two extremes is a difficult proposition—it is akin to walking a minefield. Yet, such negotiations are absolutely necessary if we as scholars and teachers are serious in our commitment to furthering knowledge—a category different from information. Negotiating the space between erasure and appropriation is also an important part of our responsibility to our students in providing structures for their own investigations. It is with this understanding that this study is undertaken, a study that is at its core one of reception.

The motivation for this project grew out of an unspecified, general unease on my part in encountering a contradictory discourse within Literary Studies. On the one hand the discipline seemed to be actively seeking out so-called marginalized texts to the point of engaging in a preemptive celebration of a newfound diversity. Yet, the field is also at times engaging in blatant colonizing practices that further strengthen hegemonic centers of power. It seemed logical then to sort out these contradictions by spelling out precisely *which* Latina/o and Latin American texts were incorporated into this discourse, particularly outside of area studies and Spanish departments, as well as attempting to discover how these texts were being used in both critical and pedagogical practices. The intent was to work backward from this information ultimately to reach a point from which to theorize the process of selection and incorporation.

I approached this project much like an anthropologist, gathering data in the form of surveys, and cataloging artifacts such as calls for papers, conference proceedings, and the MLA Job List. Most importantly, I gathered field notes from my time spent among U.S. academics in their "natural" environment, the university and its surroundings. What I discovered from this type of research is that the information I was seeking is elusive and prone to a high degree of ambiguity. As I labored over the cryptic language of a call for papers on "border crossings," for example, my training in performing close readings led to frustration regarding the true meaning not only of the brief passage requesting such papers, but of practically every word contained within it. The highly specialized language of Literary Studies did not function as a means of limiting meaning but, rather, further compressed it. The harder I tried to pin it down, the more likely I was to wind up chasing scattered signification.

Intrapersonal communication in professional and pseudoprofessional settings proved slightly more useful in guiding my research. On one occasion, a faculty member mentioned that he taught a class on the short story that included Borges. Quite proud of his "global" perspective, he boasted of the profound impact this had on his students: "It just blew their minds!" When he told me the story he had assigned was "The South" ("El sur"), I was a bit surprised and commented that that particular text seemed to me, and to many others as well, to be Borges's most Argentine story. As we engaged in a discussion of the work, he interrupted me and, confused, asked, "Are we talking about the same story?" After our conversation, he seemed disappointed. He had assumed that if there was one Latin American writer he could read, and teach, without all this pesky business of context, Borges was it.

The "Borges Perplex" resurfaced when I interviewed for a position in an English department as a specialist in Latina/o literature. Everyone wanted to talk about Borges. Well, I didn't get the job. Actually, the department decided to pass up the line and assigned the Latina/o literature class to an instructor with a Ph.D. in Creative Writing and no course work, publications, or interest in Latina/o literature. So it goes.

What I started to piece together, and some would say I proved a slow learner in this respect, is that the perception seemed to be that specialized knowledge in Latin American or Latina/o literature is irrelevant, if indeed such a thing exists. Any reasonably smart person with a degree of competence in Literary Studies can write about this, and teach it as well.

This point was further illustrated by yet another encounter. A graduate student in English, with all of her course work completed, was advised to talk to me since she wanted to specialize in Latina literature, and the department had no such specialist. When we set up a lunch date I assumed she wanted feedback on her prospectus or perhaps information on hard-to-find critical materials, but what I discovered was that she had done no course work or in-depth independent research on this. She had read *The House on Mango Street* and a handful of other texts by Latinas, taken a seminar on African American literature, and felt on some level prepared to write a dissertation on Latina literature.

She, and her director, assumed that over the course of a lunch, I could somehow impart all the information needed to transform her into a Latina literature specialist. Of course, nobody would advise a student wishing to specialize in, say, Renaissance, to take a Renaissance scholar to lunch and gather all that needs to be known to write her/his dissertation in that field. All I could do was give this student a few names and wish her luck, since she seemed adamant about her plans, once again on the advice of her committee, which felt this would make her a highly marketable job candidate.

I share these narratives because they seem to bear a great deal of relevance to how Latin American and Latina/o literatures are used as additives to curricula in a process of inclusion without influence.[5] The texts themselves are too often viewed as raw material, extracted from specific locations and transported across geographic, political, and disciplinary borders for the production of knowledge in hegemonic centers. Barbara Harlow summarizes the reproduction of neocolonial relationships through scholarship in the following manner:

> Theory . . . or a regionalized construction of what constitutes theoretical work, has, like "feminism" in its most dominant modes, come to be legislated from out of the western capitals, thus giving rise to another "international division of labor," whereby the cultural raw materials are mined in the Third World and delivered to the manufacturing and processing centers of the First World where they are transformed into commodities consumed by an educated elite. (Harlow, "All That Is Inside" 168)

I would add to this statement that in our participation as manufacturers of culture through both critical and pedagogical practices, we are also engaged in illicit smuggling activities. We are, in other words, transporting dangerous cargo. Like the coyotes who transport undocumented workers across the U.S./Mexico border for profit, U.S. academics are transporting texts across borders, disciplinary and otherwise. Like coyotes, we control the route to be taken and the point of entry, and play a role in how our contraband is put to use for our own benefit and in the service of the powerful.

Recognizing our roles as analogous to that of the coyote can be challenging; after all, coyotes are despised by both the authorities policing borders as well as those individuals who must contract their services. The very name *coyote* reflects this scorn. The animal *Canis latrans* is commonly seen as a pest, "a carrion-eater, an ignoble slouching unkempt canid" (Phelan 134). Yet, the coyote identity can also have empowering possibilities which can take on ethical dimensions. *Canis latrans* may not be as majestic as its relative the wolf, but through its adaptability it has flourished, while the wolf has been driven to near extinction (Phelan 134).

Coyote's other negative attributes, that it has no regard for either property or borders, can also yield positive associations for those of us who embrace the coyote identity.[6]

But perhaps the most productive aspect of the coyote as analogous comes from its identification, in indigenous cultures of the western United States and Mexico, as a trickster figure and a shape-shifter. The coyote identity can help break down rigid notions of absolutes and fixed identities as well as our desire for "authenticity." As trickster, the coyote can guide our border crossings as we negotiate the barriers that guard institutional and disciplinary boundaries.

For undocumented workers, the stakes in border crossings are of course much higher, often a matter of life and death. My use of borders as tropes is not intended to diminish or in any way exploit the all too real, desperate situation of illegal immigrants. Yet, as I witness anti-immigration rhetoric grow into an all-out declaration of war, neatly dividing the "us" and "them," I can't help but see the parallels in academic discourse and institutional practices that tolerate certain trespassers but only under certain conditions, particularly if the interlopers could be put to use without interrogating and challenging existing structures of domination. To extend power to these cultural productions, on their own terms, would imply a loss of control over the institution's metaphoric boundaries, just as the shrillest anti-immigration voices warn may happen, or has already happened, as the nation fails to control its borders.

Because the topic of reception encompasses a multitude of factors, each of the five chapters presented here focuses on a specific aspect of the problem. Three of the chapters focus on a single text so as to allow for an in-depth analysis of the issues each text presents in relation to the reception process. Two of the chapters explore the process in a slightly different manner: from issues to texts. Although the individual chapters are written as somewhat independent units, making them readable in isolation from the work as a whole, I've attempted to follow a spiraling thematic structure cycling recurrent concerns from chapter to chapter.

Chapter 1, "Border Crossers and Coyotes," frames a discussion of the dynamics of reception that defines the larger work through an analysis of Ruth Behar's *Translated Woman: Crossing the Border with Esperanza's Story*. Because this text engages an overtly self-reflexive strategy by incorporating Esperanza's story, the story of how the book was written, and Behar's own "intellectual autobiography" and "shadow biography," it is particularly well suited to laying the foundations for a discussion of how and why marginalized texts enter into academic discourse. By performing a reading of Behar's reading of Esperanza's life narrative, the chapter addresses reception as a form of production. *Translated Woman* is particularly useful in its explanation of the power inequities between the United States and Mexico and how these relationships are relevant to crosscultural communication.

Behar's text explores what it means to be a Jewish, Cuban American, feminist anthropologist, trained in and funded by U.S. institutions of higher learning. It investigates the problematic nature of conducting research on the life of a very differently positioned woman. This exploration leads to the articulation of the role of the U.S. academic "doing work" on texts from *el otro lado,* the other side, as analogous to the role of the coyote. Within this identity, the question becomes what type of coyote we choose to be. This is the question I take up in chapters 2 through 5.

Chapter 2, "Boom(ing) Fictions: Magical Realism and the Reception of Latina/o Literatures," surveys current articulations of "magical realism" as paradigmatic of Latin American literature, particularly by critics whose fields of expertise lie outside Hispanism. The chapter relates how the "Boom" in Latin American fiction has been constructed, particularly in First World critical discourses, and the effect this construct has had on the reception of some Latina/o texts. The practice of subsuming all Latin American literature under the label of "magical realism," and the subsequent extension of the term in classifying and interpreting certain Latina/o texts, is defined here as "Booming" or the "Booming effect."

Chapter 3, "Out of Bounds: *Testimonio* and Its Reception," surveys the reception of *testimonio,* articulating and analyzing the various ways it destabilizes notions of authorship, genre, literature, and the relationship of all of these to political practices. This third chapter draws into sharper focus concerns raised in chapter 1 regarding the process of constructing, through the editing and translation process, a life narrative so as to render it recognizable as such within existing frameworks. Using *I, Rigoberta Menchú: An Indian Woman in Guatemala* [*Me llamo Rigoberta Menchú, y así me nació la conciencia*] as an exemplary *testimonio,* the chapter outlines the difficulties the text poses for the reader/critic. It calls for a revision of reading and critical strategies that could then be put into pedagogical practice by re-reading the canon through marginalized texts. This is proposed as a departure from the usual current practice of reading works such as *testimonio* through the lens of conventions established within a western literary tradition.

Chapter 4, "Spic Spanglish? The Reception of *Borderlands/La Frontera* and Linguistic Resistance," looks at the reception of Gloria Anzaldúa's hybrid autobiographical text and identifies trends that decontextualize, essentialize, exceptionalize, and universalize the work. These readings of the text are produced through a denial on the part of the reader/critic of the differential status of languages within U.S. hegemony. The chapter uses a cultural studies approach situating the reception of *Borderlands/La Frontera* within a broader set of discourses ranging from popular culture, to feminist critical and institutional practices, to theories of *mestizaje*. The chapter proposes engagement with the text through attention to the text's use of language as a site of resistance. This allows for the opening of a transformational space from which to interrogate unequal power relations based on race, gender, class, and sexualities.

The final chapter, "Coming of Age in the Curriculum: *The House on Mango Street* and *Bless Me, Ultima* as Representative Texts," attempts to plot the location of the uses of these works, as representative texts, on the multicultural matrix. This matrix is composed of various forms of multiculturalism defined by critics according to the varying philosophical, ideological, and political presuppositions and agendas that undergird each position. The chapter argues that these two texts have become legal trespassers on the academic landscape. Their legal status is based at least partly on their high degree of intelligibility, which allows for the reader to interpret the text outside of its specific context. A second factor in these texts having "crossed over" is the ability of academic discourse to contain their oppositional potential through "manageable difference."

That both these texts can be read as forms of the bildungsroman, or coming-of-age novel, is posited as particularly influential in their reception, as is the fact that they are narrated through the voices of children. By studying the reception of two texts that have moved, at least to some degree, from periphery to center, this chapter approaches the coyote question not at the time of crossing, as do the other chapters, but after the fact.

I hope that this study will prove useful to students, teachers, and scholars who share an interest in border-crossing texts. Although such texts can, indeed, be dangerous cargo, engagement with them is necessary given that they are situated in a zone that will increasingly come to define the twenty-first century "marked by borrowing and lending across porous national and cultural boundaries that are saturated with inequality, power, and domination" (Rosaldo, *Culture* 217). The primary objective of this book is to further the discussion regarding multiculturalism and the role of the humanities in crosscultural communication, yet I also hope that it will spark internal debates within individuals. While the central argument presented here—namely, that in our roles as teachers and scholars we function as coyotes transporting potentially dangerous cargo—may seem a condemnation of our work, I hope that it will ultimately be embraced as an identity full of possibilities.

1

Border Crossers and Coyotes

There is no neutral standpoint in the power-laden field of discursive positionings, in a shifting matrix of relationships, of *I*'s and *you*'s.

James Clifford, *The Predicament of Culture*

down in the bowels
of the brick building
Esperanza's words come out
clean, neat, pretty
permanent-pressed on white paper
folded into fresh plastic bags
with zip-lock tops.

Ruth Behar, *Translated Woman*

How does a scholar, affiliated with and supported by U.S. institutions, go about gathering the life story of a Mexican woman—racially and economically marginalized within her own society—so as to put that story into book form to be consumed by an academic audience in the United States? This is the story Ruth Behar weaves into the text of *Translated Woman: Crossing the Border with Esperanza's Story.* The subtitle directs the reader to the role the researcher's own story will play in the book. The main title is also used to refer to both Esperanza and Behar. The latter's positionality—or identification—as a Jewish, Cuban American woman is problematized in the text. The book is as much Esperanza's life story as the story of how the book was written, including chapters on theory and methodology as well as the researcher's "intellectual autobiography" and a "shadow biography."[1]

The term *shadow biography* refers to Behar's own biography or life story, which exists and develops alongside the life story that she is collecting, that of Esperanza. This overtly self-reflexive strategy renders an analysis of *Translated Woman* useful in laying the foundations for a discussion of how and why marginalized texts enter into academic discourse, as well as our own participation as teachers and scholars in these border crossings. This study proposes that our roles align us with the figure of the coyote, the person who transports undocumented workers across the U.S./Mexico border for profit. While the coyote is despised by the workers he/she transports as well as, for very different reasons, the "documented" inhabitants of the states, this study proposes that identification with this figure can help us recognize the pitfalls in our work, namely negotiating the space between appropriation and erasure. It furthermore suggests ways to transform our coyote identity into positive action in terms of both research and pedagogical practices.

A discussion of the coyote as analogous to the work of U.S. academics in terms of both scholarship and pedagogical practices necessitates a preliminary discussion of the border and how it is being theorized. To do this, it is imperative to situate Behar's *Translated Woman* as well as this entire study in the field(s) of Border Studies and Border Theory. Border Studies focuses on a specific geographic location, the U.S./Mexico border. It aims to articulate and analyze not only geopolitical relations between the two nations as they manifest themselves on the region and its inhabitants, but also cultural productions on both sides, which grow out of the historic and daily realities shaped by the existence of the border. Border Theory, pioneered by Chicana/o intellectuals, similarly centers on the U.S./Mexico border, but also envisions the border as a condition. As such, the borderlands become descriptive, not only of that space between Mexico and the United States, but also of its multiple duplications, which take place within and between subjects and discourses.

David E. Johnson and Scott Michaelsen, editors of the collection of essays *Border Theory*, cite Gloria Anzaldúa's *Borderlands/La Frontera: The New Mestiza* (1987), Renato Rosaldo's *Culture and Truth: The Remaking of Social Analysis* (1989), D. Emily Hicks's *Border Writing: The Multidimensional Text* (1991), Héctor Calderón and José David Saldívar's essay collection *Criticism in the Borderlands* (1991), and Ruth Behar's *Translated Woman* (1993) as "influential works" in the field of Border Studies and Border Theory (Johnson and Michaelsen 1). We could add to this list José David Saldívar's *Border Matters: Remapping American Cultural Studies* (1997), Guillermo Gomez-Peña's *Warrior for Gringostroika* (1993), and Sonia Saldívar-Hull's *Feminism on the Border: Chicana Gender Politics and Literature* (2000). There have also been influential articles by critics such as Yvonne Yarbro-Bejarano, Carl Gutierrez-Jones, George

Yúdice, and Juan Flores, to name but a few. Border Studies and Border Theory have also been developing on the Mexican side of the border. Néstor García Canclini's *Culturas Híbridas* (1989) [*Hybrid Cultures*], for example, is a particularly influential text.[2] Noting these titles' publication dates, we could surmise that the field is, institutionally speaking, in its infancy. This work, rooted primarily in Chicana/o studies, has also been in active dialogue with work in other fields, such as that of Homi Bhabha, Abdul JanMohamed, and Mary Louise Pratt.[3]

Through this ongoing work, the border (traditionally envisioned as the outer fringe) has been redrawn at the center. As Flores and Yúdice propose, in their article "Living Borders/Buscando América," the U.S. map has been culturally redrawn as an America that is all border. Furthermore, Border Theory has also subverted the notion of the border as the limit that defines and contains the nation, and transformed it rather into a space that not only allows for but necessitates global connectedness. José David Saldívar summarizes this point in writing, "The invocation of the U.S.-Mexico border as a paradigm of crossing, resistance, and circulation in Chicano/a studies has contributed to the 'worldling' of American studies and further helped to instill a new transnational literacy in the U.S. academy" (Saldívar, *Border* xiii).

The figure of the scholar/teacher as coyote can help us define our own positions and roles in this new academic terrain. Behar's *Translated Woman*, as discussed in this chapter, illustrates both the border crossings that texts undergo as they enter academic discourse as well as our own participation, as coyotes, in these border crossings.

The first and most obvious transformation of Esperanza's story, or its first border crossing, is its movement from the oral to the written. This process of textualization, however obvious, is everything but simple. It has been argued by critics such as Derrida in his deconstruction of logocentrism—or the privileging of the spoken word over the written—that all language mediates, the very act of language deferring meaning. In the essay, "Plato's Pharmacy," Derrida subsumes speech as a form of writing. Even if we accept this scriptocentric position, it is still true that as a form of writing, the oral tale is quite different from the written.[4] Even a transcript of an oral tale becomes something else. By necessity, "reading" in the literal sense is a different process from that of "listening," just as "writing" is different from "speech." Behar as editor is fully aware of her roles as both listener to Esperanza's storytelling and author of that story by "retelling" it in written form.

> It worries me that one does violence to the life history as a story by turning it into the disposable commodity of information. One approach I took to this problem was to focus on the act of life story representation as reading rather than as informing, with its echoes of surveillance and disclosures of truth. I have tried to make clear that what I am reading is a story, or set of stories, that have been told to me, so that I, in turn, can tell them again, transforming myself from a listener into a storyteller. (Behar, *Translated Woman* 13)

The use of the word *storyteller* is significant in that it masks the fact that in having to "cut, cut, and cut away at our talk to make it fit between the covers of a book, and even more important, to make it recognizable *as a story,* a certain kind of story, a life history" (Behar 12), Behar has assumed a role that, if perhaps not entirely the author's, strongly resembles it. The construct of author implies the story be fixed as text, conforming in some way to a recognizable form; that is, we must recognize it as a story. Even the most experimental text presents itself as belonging to a particular genre, for to push or to put into question the boundaries of form we must first agree that such a form, along with its boundaries, exists.

To cast Behar as the author of another woman's story is not intended here as criticism of her work. To expect the subaltern to speak, in terms of a written text which can then enter the realm of academic discourse, is a utopian ideal, as Gayatri Spivak reminds us.[5] What makes *Translated Woman* a particularly interesting text is that it drops the curtain that usually conceals the process of collaborative texts, be they anthropological in nature, ethnographies, or autobiography and *testimonio.* In doing so, *Translated Woman* avoids "treating the 'author' of the 'testimonial' as an authentic, singular voice without acknowledging the mediations of the editors and market demands of publishing" which, Caren Kaplan warns, "can result in new forms of exoticization and racism" (Kaplan 122).

Translated Woman, rather than fostering the illusion of an unmediated first-person narrative, upholds what Carole Boyce Davies identifies as the "oral narrative contract" in life story telling. Davies writes:

> In the oral narrative process, "trust" is often fostered when the editor supplies features of her own life story. The narrating takes place then in a context of plural identity and shared history. In the written version, however, it seems, the oral life narrating contract is often violated. Rarely is the collector's story part of the narrative. At the point of writing, then, the dominant-subordinate relationships are en-

> forced and the editor becomes a detached, sometimes clinical, orderer or even exploiter of the life stories for anthropological ends, research data, raw material, or the like. (Davies 12–13)

By writing herself into the narrative, or rather resisting writing herself out, Behar can avert the more obvious trappings of colonizing Esperanza's story. By including her story in the text, Behar also intensifies our awareness as readers of how and to what extent every subject participates in the historical, economic, political, and cultural set of relations implicated in a narrative that is displaced across borders for the purpose of consumption in an academic marketplace.

Behar chooses to use "both a novelistic style and a dialogical style in this book," so as to "keep Esperanza's voice at the center of the text" (Behar, *Translated Woman* 14). The choice reflects the changes over time in the relationship between the two women. Behar also makes explicit use of other forms such as drama, as when she introduces one of Esperanza's monologues with stage directions: "July 13, 1988. At the kitchen table again after another year's absence. Same cast of characters" (179).[6] And by the final chapters of *Translated Woman,* prose is disrupted by poetry. This blending of forms is arguably a daring choice that make the book that much harder to define. In her preface, Behar posits a measure of success for this project in terms of its ability to reflect the complexity and contradictions that mark Esperanza's life and her story. She states, "If nothing else, I hope I've made her life in this book too big for easy consumption" (xii). Her narrative strategies do just that.

The first part of Esperanza's story, beginning with her birth and leading up to the present time, is narrated through recreated monologues that read as a testimonial novel. It is told in the first person, with the use of dialogue, an element that Behar notes reflects Esperanza's own style, "telling virtually the entire story in dialogue form, changing voices like a spirit medium or a one-woman theater of voices to impersonate all the characters in her narratives" (Behar, *Translated Woman* 7). This "novelistic style" also reflects Esperanza's own narrative models, noted by Behar as being Christian narratives of redemption, *fotonovelas,*[7] confessional narratives, and "myths of women warriors, such as those found in the colonial Mexican Inquisition narratives" (12).[8] It serves as a warning to our essentializing drive to note that ascribing purity in terms of influences, even when the storyteller does not have access to the technology of literacy, is an act of nostalgia. The culture of writing has so permeated outward to influence other forms that, while maintaining its difference from written texts, oral storytelling in contemporary contexts often reflects literary models that have been filtered through mass media.

The novelistic style of this first portion of Esperanza's life story conforms to the genre's seamless claim to "reality." It adheres to literary expectations of character, plot, chronology, conflict, and so on. Interestingly, this style's appeal to us readers lies in the contradiction that because it is highly stylized, and follows literary models, it becomes believable as truth. How this effect is achieved is quite complicated and well beyond the scope of this book, demanding an analysis of that blurred space between fiction and nonfiction. This is the very space that has been the subject of debate within disciplines such as anthropology and history in the recent past, as well as at the core of much of the Latin American fiction that has established itself as "canonical." Works by Borges, Carpentier, García Márquez, and Fuentes, to name just a few, enter and explore this liminal space from the opposite side of autobiographical narrative. But liminal spaces such as this are borderlands, and as we enter, disorientation takes over. Because of this, approaching the blurred space between fiction and nonfiction, from the perspective of either, leads us to similar questions. Thus, by extension, to explore this borderland we should enter from both sides, or more accurately, from a multiplicity of sides.

In Part Two of the book, Esperanza's story narrates the here and now in the context of her evolving relationship with Behar. The "gringa anthropologist"—a label Behar uses and later in the text subverts—is an active participant in these chapters. She ventures out alongside her *comadre* on her selling routes, visiting her *comadre's milpa,* and even accompanying her to a ceremony at a spiritist center venerating the—then problematic for Behar—figure of Pancho Villa.[9] In these chapters, as opposed to those constituting Part One, we hear Behar's voice directly through dialogue and narration. The visit to the spiritist center becomes a turning point, both in the relationship between Behar and Esperanza and in the text—it is placed, not coincidentally, in the physical center of the book. The events that transpire at the center are described as part fiesta, part religious ceremony, and part performance orchestrated by the Centro's leader, Chencha, speaking as the medium for the voice of General Francisco Villa. The fiesta has been described by the Mexican poet and essayist Octavio Paz as a public celebration that sanctions transgression and subversion of the status quo. During the fiesta, participants can assume alternate identities and disrupt the otherwise rigid hierarchies of class, race, and gender.[10] This is precisely what happens under Chencha's direction.

The visit to the spiritist center is pivotal. From that point onward the relationship between Esperanza and Behar becomes more complicated and layered, moving beyond that of anthropologist/informant. It even moves beyond that of *comadres,* which in Mexico, particularly in rural areas, is still marked by a certain distance and formality although it is structured to not only allow for but encourage relationships among women that transgress class divisions.[11]

The narrative style in these chapters reflects Behar's negotiations of a heightened awareness of her own position or rather her multiple positionings in relation to Esperanza and the evolving narrative of her/their life stories. Gone is the seamless literariness of the previous section. In its place are stop-and-start dialogues and moments of authorial interruption offering interpretations of events only to later put those interpretations into question. By the end of Part Two, *Translated Woman* is a fragmented, multivoiced text.

Through the events described in these chapters, Behar begins to see "how Esperanza's historias fit into the fuller context of her life" (Behar, *Translated Woman* 13). She also gains a broader understanding of how their relationship fits into the contexts of anthropology as a discipline, U.S./Mexico relations, transnational feminism, and class differences. Interestingly, as fuller contexts are developed, what ensues is a greater degree of disorder, rather than order. This reflects a discernable uneasiness in Behar and, by extension, in the reader as we become complicitous in Behar's project as consumers of her book. This heightened anxiety regarding positionalities, power relations, and contradictions reflects Edward Said's observation that "it seems a common human failing to prefer the schematic authority of a text to the disorientation of encounters with the human" (Said 93). The complexity of what it means to have one woman, from north of the border, gather and translate another woman's story for circulation *del otro lado* is reproduced thematically and stylistically in these chapters.

The assertion that *Translated Woman* as a text moves from order to disorder, paralleling the maturing relationship between the two women, is also indicative of Behar's struggle in relinquishing rather than solidifying her interpretative power over Esperanza's narrative. This movement toward disorder, it must be noted, goes counter to what Clifford defines as the "approved *topoi* for the portrayal of the research process" within the field of anthropology. Behar inverts the "more-or-less stereotypic 'fables of rapport' [which] narrate the attainment of full participant status" (Clifford 40). According to Clifford,

> These fables may be told elaborately or in passing, naively or ironically. They normally portray the ethnographer's early ignorance, misunderstanding, lack of contact—frequently a sort of child-like status within the culture. In the *Bildungsgeschichte* of the ethnography these states of innocence or confusion are replaced by adult, confident, disabused knowledge. . . . [the pivotal anecdote] establishes a presumption of connectedness, which permits the writer to function in his [her] subsequent analyses as an omnipresent, knowledgeable exegete and spokesman. . . . [the anthropologist's] disappearance into his [her] rapport—the quasi-invisibility of participant observation—is paradigmatic. (Clifford 40–41)

If we take Behar's visit to the spiritist center as the pivotal event in her relationship with Esperanza, we can see that in contrast to the researcher emerging as an authority by essentially writing the dialogical nature of her work out of the text, Behar emerges as a more problematized presence. Her privileged position as the "reader" of the event is brought into question. Her participation in the performance, scripted and directed by Chencha, involves gathering three pesos, from three different purses, to present as an offering. Yet because the peso had gone through a series of severe devaluations, the one peso coin had been rendered obsolete. As Behar realizes, Chencha's making her beg for three coins, whose value has been reduced to nothing due to global economic exchanges in which the United States plays a major role, inverts the relation of power between the "gringa anthropologist" and the other participants at the *centro*. Rather than writing herself out of the events she seeks to interpret, Behar highlights how she cannot escape her scripted positionings. Her interpretative authority becomes, through her own writing, suspect.

The inclusion in Part Three of various anecdotes relating to photography provides for a concrete rendering of Behar and Esperanza's positioning in a history of images of "the other" crossing borders, a history wrought with conflict, exploitation, commodification, and an exoticizing of "the other." When Behar casually mentions that she is finally able to photograph Esperanza with her calla lilies, we are invited to make the comparison between this second moment and their first encounter. The second opportunity to photograph Esperanza takes place in her garden, made possible by her explicit invitation. This is in sharp contrast to Behar's first encounter with Esperanza, which also involved photography, as described in the introduction. Behar writes, "She was striking. She held a bulging bouquet of calla lilies and seemed to me like something out of one of Diego Rivera's epic Indian woman canvases. . . . I jumped on her as an alluring image of Mexican womanhood, ready to create my own exotic portrait of her" (Behar 4).

This description of the first framing of Esperanza in the anthropologist/photographer's lens is consciously pointed out as problematic and in sharp contrast to the reframing of Esperanza with calla lilies that occurs years later. There is no question that the two photo opportunities are strikingly different. The latter provides a context that is specific—Esperanza is *a* woman in her garden, which is her source of income and tangible proof of her hard-won independence. In contrast, the first photo totalizes, positing Esperanza as *the* Mexican Woman, resulting in an exoticizing and colonizing image.

Yet, even this second, more contextualized photograph is problematic in that it can't escape participation in the history of "photographing the other," nor can it suspend the asymmetry of power between photographer and subject and the commodification of the image. Behar's casual mention of this second photograph, and her directing the reader to the former, more obviously loaded framing seems to be a denial of how she and her work are entangled in this history. And Behar almost succeeds in getting herself off the hook, were it not for a hyperawareness of her conflicted position, revealed in two other anecdotes relating to photography.

In the chapter titled, "Gringa Sings the Blues," Behar agonizes over the townspeople's perception of her and her work, and "determined to be blue," asks her *comadre,* "Tell me again what your mama said about the photographs I took of her" (Behar 251). Esperanza then relates her mother's dissatisfaction with the photographs, which she feels made her look "All dark . . . with the garbage of papers around her" (Behar 251). More importantly, Esperanza's mother expresses suspicion about Behar's motives. "Why do they go around taking pictures? They take them back and they make money off them. Here one's a ranchero, and they take our pictures and give them to those people who make calendars and they earn their money. And there your compadres go, too. Why do you think they're here taking photographs?" (Behar 252).

Esperanza's mother, Doña Nicolasa, makes her suspicions regarding

Behar's work even clearer by comparing her to two men who years earlier had offered to pay her and Esperanza for photographing them. Doña Nicolasa had refused, saying "No, Señor, we are what we are, but we don't go around selling ourselves for money" (Behar 253). The anecdote parallels Behar's experience a few days earlier, during a town fiesta, when a man pressured her into taking photographs of him and demanded payment. Her reflections on the experience—"I knew that my interaction with that man inscribed a certain history of Westerners photographing others, in which those others were now seizing, if not the cameras, at least some of the power involved in snapping their pictures" (Behar 253)—demonstrate that an awareness of the history connecting exploitation and photography, and even applauding resistance to it, does not automatically make one innocent in these exchanges, no matter how noble one's intentions.

Behar's reaction to Doña Nicolasa's indirect accusations is also revealing. She writes,

> I had to admit . . . that I was impressed by Doña Nicolasa's knowledge of a market for photographs of exotic others and her resistance toward being a part of it, even if I resented being placed in the same category as the men who had stopped them on the highway. Her refusal to be objectified or commodified by men was admirable in every way—except when I felt implicated. And how could I doubt that I was implicated—hadn't my first encounter with Esperanza been a photographic one? (Behar 254)

Behar's unease in confronting Doña Nicolasa's interpretation of her motives for wielding a camera lies in the fact that the nature of her work places her in the slippery position of standing in opposition to the history of exploitation, but only by working within hegemonic systems that she may inadvertently be perpetuating.

Further complicating this already complex set of historical relationships is Behar's approach to her work from a gendered perspective, identifying herself as a feminist anthropologist. The relationship between the two women, and the text they collaboratively produce, are part of yet another context, that of transnational feminism. As a feminist, Behar can admire Doña Nicolasa's "refusal to be objectified and commodified by men" and can even claim to identify with the two women; but because her work places her on the opposite side of the lens, her position is more closely aligned with that of the male photographers. Behar is then negotiating yet another slippery space that carries its own dangers.

Chandra Talpade Mohanty has pointed out that certain Western feminist practices engage in a form of "discursive colonization" that invokes an "appropriation and commodification of 'scholarship' and 'knowledge' about women in the Third World" by employing particular analytic categories "which take as their referent feminist interests as they have been articulated in the U.S. and Western Europe" (Mohanty 333–34). Behar demonstrates a keen awareness of this potential for colonizing, the seductive lure of positing Third World women as the mirror image of First World feminists, where we can see ourselves through distortions as implicitly "educated, modern, as having control of [our] own bodies and sexualities, and the freedom to make [our] own decisions" (Mohanty 337).

Behar identifies contradictions in Esperanza's stories that are irreconcilable with her own feminism. She finds beating her daughter—once for not telling her about her half-brother making sexual advances, and another time for not giving her a share of her earnings as a maid—intelligible, yet nonetheless problematic. Esperanza's beating of the woman who was having an affair with her husband is equally, if not more, troubling to Behar. And Esperanza's participation in the spiritist cult venerating the super-macho figure of Pancho Villa is given a great deal of attention, including a variety of interpretations that ultimately seem to be exercises demonstrating Behar's need to fit the pieces neatly together.

What Behar comes to realize is that a life is rarely "a well wrought urn," and when interpretive paradigms cross borders—be they cultural, geographic, racial, or economic—the inadequacy of those paradigms is either brought into question, or quite simply the pieces are forced to fit, at any cost. Behar chooses the former, aiming to "work the dialectic between Esperanza's no-name feminism and my feminism of too many names, to go beyond the search for heroines on either side of the border" (Behar 276). This approach enables her to question her own authority over interpretation and ask "From whose perspective, whose absolute scale of feminist perfection, are her attitudes and actions being measured?" (Behar 296). She can even conclude,

> That I can now call myself a feminist ethnographer and this book a work of feminist ethnography does not mean, however, that I am "more" of a feminist than Esperanza. If anything I am "less" of a feminist, I who have sought to see the patriarchy in Esperanza's life through the lens of a patriarchal discipline, I who have crossed the border as an employee of a patriarchal academic corporation, I who

> have been so generously patronized by the inheritances of men who in their lifetimes made enough money to create foundations in their names. (Behar 302)

By questioning her own positionality, Behar is engaging in a critique of objectivity and by extension a critique of scholarship itself. She is, like other feminist scholars described by Lila Abu-Lughod, "reclaim[ing] and redefin[ing] objectivity to mean precisely the situated view. There is no such thing as a study which is not situated, [she] would argue" (Abu-Lughod 15). Behar's multiple selves, as a Jewish, Cuban American woman, are consistently highlighted, subverting the subject/object, self/other dichotomy that assumes a unified and uncontested self or, as many critics have argued, provides the illusion of the unified and uncontested self in relation to "the other."[12] She observes that "There's something about being on the border that is unsettling. Something about having your belongings open for inspection. Something about having to declare who you are, what country you owe allegiance to. Something about having to pretend your identity is not already in question" (Behar 227).

Behar's self-consciousness allows her to see how her own practices entangle her in "webs of betrayal . . . seeking out intimacy and friendship with subjects on whose backs, ultimately, the books will be written upon which . . . productivity . . . in the academic marketplace will be assessed" (Behar 297). Sliding back and forth between languages, cultures, national borders, and ideologies, Behar becomes, along with Esperanza, a "translated woman." But, unlike Esperanza, she is the translator, and as such must confront the all too present danger of becoming a Malinche. Referred to as "the tongue," Malintzín, or Malinche, was Hernan Cortez's concubine and translator.[13] She has been scripted in a broad range of discourses, from historical narratives to popular culture, as the ultimate traitor. Contemporary Mexican and Chicana feminists have offered alternative interpretations of this enigmatic woman, what she represents, and how she is represented, but the associations between "traddutora, traditora" are still close to the surface.[14] For Behar, the conflict comes down to "whether one can in fact ever represent a counter project while being funded, housed and incorporated within the system" (Sánchez, "Ethnicity" 84).

Behar's questioning of her own overdetermined "feminism of too many names," however, as a strategy of resistance, by itself, is still an incomplete recognition of Esperanza's "no-name feminism." As Lynn Phillips, quoted by Behar, points out, the acceptance of many feminisms "means giving up our power to define what feminism is" (Behar 297). Acknowledging this, Behar does articulate Esperanza's feminism, even as she admits her inability to make it compatible with her own.

First and foremost, Behar facilitates Esperanza's story, mediated as it is, so that as readers we may draw our own interpretations. She also offers interpretations of Esperanza's life story that recognize her difference and point out how apparently paradoxical positions such as Esperanza's appropriation "of culturally male values that oppress her as well as other women in order to liberate and redeem herself" can also be interpreted as feminist practices in that

> Esperanza's struggle to define herself, through gender and in spite of gender, ambiguously gendered rather than passively gendered, points the way to the possibility of true gender transformation. So does her struggle to make herself whole, to be self and other, "woman" and "man," in the face of metonymic representation that would reduce her to the insignificant partness of being only a subjugated female. (Behar 296)

Esperanza's performance of motherhood can also be interpreted as feminist practice. In a culture that formulates motherhood as the only means, for a woman, of attaining recognition, Esperanza resists sentimentalizing her role as a mother. For forcing her son out of her house, she is perceived by the other townspeople, particularly the women, as a "bad mother." Ironically, as Esperanza reveals to Behar, she kicks her son out of the house to protect her daughter, whom he was molesting. By valorizing her daughter over her son, Esperanza transforms motherhood into an act of resistance, and for that, she pays a price.

Perhaps Esperanza's feminism is most clearly seen in her embracing of *coraje*, an emotion similar to rage. It is this *coraje* that Esperanza cites as motivation for telling her story, and she advises her *comadre* Behar to write what she wants, but with *coraje*. This emotion, powerful enough to dry up her milk when she was nursing one of her children, gave her the strength to leave her husband. It also gave her the courage to refuse "to keep quiet about the violence that was enacted upon her body" by her father and her husband. And for this she also pays a price. Thus, although Esperanza's feminism has no name, it is certainly one that has made her not only a survivor, but an agent of change within her own life, and an influence on Behar, the feminist of "too many names" as well. She writes, "My comadre taught me quite a lot about expressing *coraje*. . . . There's plenty of *coraje* here, about being a woman, about anthropology, about United States policy toward undocumented Mexicans; some of the *coraje* is my comadre's, some of it is mine, and some of it belongs to both of us" (Behar xii).

The metamorphosis of Esperanza's story as it is mediated by the editing process, translation, and border crossings, as well as Behar's own role in this transformation, are explored in *Translated Woman*. This exploration and articulation of the roles played by the editing process, which is in turn influenced by market demands and embedded in histories and contexts of asymmetrical power relations, can be expanded to also bear relevance to the role of the critic/teacher who carries texts across borders into the realm of academic discourse. The following lines, taken from the chapter titled "Literary Wetback," illustrate Behar's struggle with her own role as the transporter of Esperanza's story:

> Just as rural Mexican laborers export their bodies for labor on American soil, Esperanza has given me her story for export only. Her story, she realizes, is a kind of commodity that will have a value on the other side that it doesn't have at home; why else would I be "using up" my life to write about her life? She has chosen to be a literary wetback, and I am to act as her literary broker, the border-crosser who will take her story to the other side and make it heard in translation. The question will be whether I can act as her literary broker without becoming the worse kind of coyote, getting her across, but only by exploiting her lack of power to make it to *el otro lado* any other way. (Behar 234)

In these lines, Esperanza's story becomes the "wetback," leaving Behar the role of coyote, a role from which she instinctively tries to distance herself. Her first auto-defining label is that of "literary broker," which carries far lighter ethical baggage than the despised "coyote." Her next association, found later in the chapter, while assumed in full recognition of its irony and problematic implications, is that of "literary prince" for Esperanza, "promising a Cinderella ending to her story by turning it into print" (Behar 244). This association comes from Esperanza's own expectations of her story finding a sympathetic audience *del otro lado*, something she knows she cannot expect from her own community in Mexquitic, which labels her a witch and otherwise judges her harshly.

But even "literary prince" is discarded and the association with the coyote reasserts itself as Behar observes that "Crossing the border by means of her story offers a hope for liberation—the remaking of herself in her own image—but that hope is embedded in the understanding that Mexicans are treated harshly and cruelly in the same place she hopes her other self will unfold. The terms of exchange are neither transparent nor easy for Esperanza, and they are not for me either" (Behar 245).

The "terms of exchange" these lines allude to, while not transparent, are nonetheless real. They become in some sense not only the price paid to the coyote for her/his services but also the subsequent "dues" to be paid once the undocumented worker/text crosses the border. For Esperanza's story, or any other text that crosses this/these border(s), it may mean exploitation in the form of appropriation or erasure in the form of dismissal.

For Behar, these "terms of exchange" solidly link her to the coyote. After all, she does stand to profit from the border crossing by way of professional advancement. Accepting the association with the coyote as part of these terms is not easy. This identification is particularly resonant given Behar's own positional relationship, as a Cuban American, Jewish woman, to academia. She too is, in a way different from Esperanza's story and Mexican laborers, a trespasser. Like a coyote, who is more often than not a Latino/a, Behar is a border dweller. She is not entirely the "gringa anthropologist" but still a "documented" participant in the hegemonic discursive area known as academia.

It is this articulation of her position as both "documented" and "trespasser" that Behar explores in the final chapter of *Translated Woman*. It is interesting that much of the criticism of the book has centered on controversy regarding this very chapter, titled "Biography in the Shadow." The chapter's opening lines bear the tone of a forced confession: "Okay, so technically speaking, I'm not a gringa. I'm Cubana, born in Cuba, raised in a series of noisy apartments in the sad boroughs of Queens, New York, that smelled of my mother's sofrito" (Behar 320). It goes on to detail her progression into a position of authority, namely that of an academic, including a specific account of her acquisition of tenure.

The first part of the chapter, which is essentially Behar's "writing back" to her professors, bears similarities to other texts of anthropology and ethnography, primarily José Limón's *Dancing with the Devil: Society and Cultural Poetics in Mexican-American South Texas* (1994) and Renato Rosaldo's *Culture and Truth* (1989).[15] Both of these texts include descriptions and analysis of the author's coming to authority within their disciplines. Both also argue that their perspectives as Chicanos and border subjects cannot be considered as falling outside of their work. Thus, Behar's inclusion of an account of her experience in acquiring a "formal education," and even her overt discussion of her own position in relation to her work, do not make her work exceptional. Rather, they align it with some of the work currently being produced by cultural critics whose research overlaps with, and in many ways defines, Border Theory.

What does make Behar's work exceptional, or at least push the limits of a "biography in the shadow," and what has brought on the harshest criticism, is the inclusion of her negotiations for a faculty position and tenure. The most direct criticism of that material appeared in a "Point of View" essay by Daphne Patai in *The Chronicle of Higher Education*, which called for an end to "nouveau solipsism." For Patai, Behar's chapter "Biography in the Shadow" served as an example of overly self-involved and self-serving scholarship.[16] Patai is not the only scholar questioning the necessity of including personal narratives within "professional" boundaries. Behar's inclusion of her own struggles can and has been perceived as a misplaced complaint, particularly in light of the fact that she has been by conventional definitions a "successful" scholar, a recipient of the MacArthur "Genius" Grant, among others, and presently holds the rank of full professor at the University of Michigan.

Patai's criticism of Behar's chapter is, to a certain point, justifiable, and even Behar herself addresses, in her book *The Vulnerable Observer* (1996), what, if anything, is gained by including highly personal narratives within one's work. Yet, for the purpose of this particular study, Behar's "Biography in the Shadow" and its surrounding controversy prove particularly useful.

Behar's battle for a faculty position and tenure at Michigan centered on whether or not she could be classified as a Latina, and therefore eligible for consideration as a minority hire. Because her grandparents were Jewish European immigrants to Cuba, she was defined as "not an authentic enough Latina" (Behar 332). However, after being awarded the MacArthur grant, she was not only hired but able to negotiate tenure as a prior condition for acceptance. The irony in this, for Behar, is that after joining the faculty, she "was immediately tabulated into the list of new minority hires" (Behar 335).

Connecting her own experiences in academia to her role as a researcher, she concludes: "Fresh from the horror of being a translated woman, I would now turn around and translate another woman for consumption on this side of the border" (Behar 335). The phrase "this side of the border," by which Behar probably means the United States, can also be interpreted to be this side of the border delineating academic discourse or even the space of authority within that discourse. The "translated woman" in these lines refers to Behar, who "translates herself" throughout the process of attaining a "formal education" and becoming a part of academic culture. In addition, however, she is also "translated" or defined and interpreted institutionally. Given this, but suppressing her own translation of Esperanza's story, Behar comes to align her position with that of the "literary wetback." She concludes that "It is not just Esperanza, then, who is a literary wetback. Even though I have borne her story across to the other side of the border, I recognize that I, too, in quite a different way, am a literary wetback in the world of academic letters, a wetback despite the papers that tell me I'm okay, I'm in, I'm a legal alien" (Behar 340).

Arguably, the term *literary wetback* does not truly apply to Behar.[17] Her role as the "translator of another woman for consumption on this side" more closely aligns her with the coyote, and her status as legal trespasser resonates as the coyote is more often than not him/herself a border dweller, simultaneously not fully belonging on either side but part of both sides.

Contrary to Behar's formulations in defining her role in relation to Esperanza's story, first as "literary broker," then as "literary prince," and finally as "literary wetback," the question is not whether she will become a coyote at all, but rather what kind of coyote. This question must also be addressed by critics, as we transport texts that are "undocumented" across the invisible borders constructed through time to guard the canon. Some texts are easily smuggled, others are more "alien" and are stopped at the gate. As critics, we must first recognize our own participation in these border crossings, and our own conflicted positionings as coyotes. There is also in this association a recognition that our roles can mark us as trespassers ourselves, and the journey, while one certainly worth taking, can pose some dangers. The question then becomes what type of coyotes we choose to be.

2

Boom(ing) Fictions

Magical Realism and the Reception of Latina/o Literatures

> I want to see Gabriel García Márquez in 3–D
> a post-posty rendition of Castañeda
> holographic shamans flying onstage
> political massacres on multiple screens
> . . . what's wrong with you pre-technological creatures?!
> *Guillermo Gómez-Peña, "Border Brujo"*

Without a doubt, the most popular Latin American novel in the United States is *One Hundred Years of Solitude* [*Cien años de soledad*] and its author, Gabriel García Márquez, the most well-known Latin American writer. This novel is so exceptionally popular that *One Hundred Years of Solitude* and Cervantes's *Don Quixote* "are the only books written in Spanish to have found a companion volume in the MLA series of guides to teaching 'World Literature.'" (Santana 17). García Márquez's name is often mentioned alongside that other great cultural export from the region, Jorge Luis Borges. Both of these authors' short stories are heavily anthologized and routinely taught in undergraduate English courses. Their names and works are also associated with the phenomenon referred to as the "Boom," although critics are still debating whether Borges's work falls under that classification or predates it. What most critics can agree on is that Borges influenced the Boom writers, and his fiction shares many of the elements associated with Boom fiction.

A generic definition of the Boom covers a rather brief period of time, from the early 1960s to the 1970s, during which there was a veritable explosion—hence the term—of literary production, specifically fiction, by Latin American writers.[1] This "explosion" was large enough to be recognized on the international cultural market. These authors, it seemed, were doing something different, and doing it in a way that readers based in metropolitan centers found intriguing.[2] They wrote of exotic places, strange occurrences, cyclically returning history, and the narrative process itself. All of this was carried out in tight, hypercrafted plot lines, in language as lush and fertile as the landscapes they described.[3]

The word used to describe this outburst of literary talent—the Boom—implies surprise and suddenness. William Gass explores the nuances of the term in the following lines:

> The critics have called it "the boom." As in "business is booming." As in "What a loud racket!" As in a cannon shot sent North. As in "blow-up," an enlargement of image which uncovers a crime. Boom as in "Big Bang," and the first milliseconds of creation. (Gass 33)

These comparisons, although intended by Gass to represent a degree of condescension on the part of critics, are nonetheless useful. The first connection, to commerce, highlights the use of Latin American literature as a commodity exchanged in the international market in much the same way as other exports, such as bananas, provide profits for multinational corporations based in the First World.[4] The next two comparisons, to disorderly noise (a loud racket) and the sound of a cannon fired, bear relation to perceptions of Latin America, and by extension its literary production, as undecipherable, chaotic, and violent.

But it is the final comparison, to "the Big Bang," that is particularly revealing. To an international readership, meaning European and American (U.S.), the Boom marked the beginning of a literature where it presumed there had been none.[5] Taking this phenomenon as the moment of creation, it is only a logical step to then make it the originating and therefore "authentic" expression of Latin America. For nonspecialists this is still a pervasively held notion. John Brushwood summarizes the stereotyping of Latin American cultural productions and its manifestations in the Boom phenomenon as follows: "For no one would accuse Europe of a boom . . . booms reverberate only from unexpected places, suddenly and sonically as if from empty air. Nothing was there before, and then BOOM!" (Brushwood 35).

Boom authors brought attention to an amorphously defined mode of representation that critics have termed, in English, magical realism. Although the term itself and works that have been classified as employing elements of magical realism predate the Boom by either a few decades or a few centuries, depending on which critical perspective one adopts, it was the Boom that brought the term into international circulation. Through a conflating of magical realism, the Boom, and the beginning of Latin American literature itself, magical realism became mistakenly established as paradigmatic of Latin America. Critics such as Steven Bell have noted that "a superficial understanding of such notions as 'magical realism' may perpetuate limiting and retrograde views of Latin America as an absolute other, as an exotic paradise or a primeval aberration" (Bell 8).[6]

The following lines by Gayatri Spivak demonstrate a critical tendency toward identifying magical realism as the definitive narrative style of Latin America. While Spivak avoids the pitfalls pointed out by Bell, the lines quoted here present a different danger in equating magical realism with the region and its cultural production. Spivak writes,

> Consider, for example, the idea that magical realism is the paradigmatic style of the third world. What is the hidden ethical, political agenda behind claiming that a style practiced most spectacularly by some writers in that part of the third world which relates most intimately with the United States, namely Latin America (just as India used to relate to Britain), is paradigmatic of a space which is trying to cope with the problem of narrativizing decolonization? In Latin American space, one of the things that cannot be narrativized is decolonization, as the Ariel-Caliban debate and today's intimate involvement with the U.S. have clearly articulated for us. (Spivak, *Outside* 13)[7]

Spivak on the one hand argues that magical realism has been misapplied as paradigmatic of the Third World. However, her opposition to the generalization of the term boils down to it being paradigmatic exclusively to Latin America, which she claims incapable of narrativizing decolonization based on its neocolonial relationship with the United States. The extent to which Latin America can, has, and is narrativizing decolonization is an issue that will have to be taken up elsewhere.[8] But Spivak's statement must still be critiqued as performing the same type of problematic generalization she is accusing other critics of doing. What makes her words particularly important is that her name as a postcolonial theorist and critic carries substantial weight, obscuring the fact that she is not a Latin Americanist.

The association between magical realism and Latin America has become so entrenched that there is a growing need to specify that the region existed prior to and outside of its being made readable by the Boom. Cuban writer Reinaldo Arenas, in his 1993 memoir, *Before Night Falls,* feels a responsibility to his readers in explaining his childhood habit of consuming dirt by pointing out: "I should make it clear right away that to eat dirt is not a metaphor, or a sensational act. All the country kids did it. It has nothing to do with magical realism or anything of the sort" (Arenas 11). Through this disclaimer, Arenas signals a point of departure from what he assumes his readers' frame of reference will be, namely the character Rebeca's lifelong indulgence in eating dirt in *One Hundred Years of Solitude.*

Further complicating the fact that magical realism, as practiced by some Boom writers, has come to be taken as paradigmatic of Latin America is the extension of the term to texts produced by Latina/o authors writing in English. While there are undoubtedly intertextual dialogues between and among Latina/o texts and those of Latin America, reader expectations have led to reductive interpretations of both. This practice of subsuming everything under the Boom can be referred to as "Boom(ing)." As a step toward sorting through these assumptions, it is imperative to first situate magical realism and the Boom in a historical and theoretical context. This can then lead to a more cogent articulation of how the conditions—historical, material, and literary—that gave rise to the Boom are different for those informing Latina/o cultural productions.

The term *magical realism,* or *Magic Realism* [*Magischer Realismus*], was first used by the German art historian Franz Roh to describe Post-Expressionist painting's return to representations of real objects while integrating elements of Expressionism. This coinage, however, had little impact in 1925, the year of its publication, since Gustav Hartlaub's competing term, New Objectivity [*Neue Sachlichkeit*], became the preferred terminology (Guenther 33). While Roh's essay lost influence in his native Germany until a renewed interest in the Weimar Republic during the 1960s exhumed it from obscurity, it had reached a broad and influential audience in the most unexpected of places: Latin America. Roh's essay, translated into Spanish and published by José Ortega y Gasset's *Revista de Occidente* in 1927, and in book form later that same year, was widely read in literary circles, and was even being discussed in relation to contemporary European prose (Guenther 61). But it was Alejo Carpentier who "Americanized" the term and argued its efficacy as a specifically American mode of expression.[9]

In the preface to his first novel, *El reino de este mundo* [*The Kingdom of this World,* 1949], Carpentier proposes the term *lo real maravilloso,* the marvelous real, as a narrative strategy born of the experience of the Americas, as opposed to the Surrealist perspective of "the marvelous, manufactured by tricks of prestidigitation, by juxtaposing objects unlikely ever to be found together" (Carpentier, "On the Marvelous" 85).[10] What Carpentier identifies as the marvelous in the Americas is the hyperbolic, the overwhelming characteristics of the landscapes, the coexistence of several historical epochs within a single frame, and the beliefs and rituals of cosmologies and mysticism that bear a different approach to the improbable, the unbelievable, the miraculous. He concludes his essay with an ontological argument for *lo real maravilloso* being a uniquely American mode of representation: "After all, what is the entire history of America if not a chronicle of the marvelous real?" (Carpentier, "On the Marvelous" 88).

Angel Flores, in a paper presented at the 1954 MLA convention, enters the debate and uses the term *magical realism* to describe a "new phase" in Latin American literature, which he marks as beginning with Jorge Luis Borges's "Historia universal de la infamia" ["A Universal History of Infamy"] published in 1935 (Flores 133). Flores's argument distances itself from Carpentier, locating the development of magical realism as a literary departure from and rebellion against the "sentimentality, . . . romantic tirades and psychological distortions" that marked classics such as *Doña Bárbara, María,* and *Aves sin nido* [*Birds without a Nest*] (Flores 110). Writing of this "new phase," Flores comments: "Their style seeks precision and leanness, a healthy innovation, to be sure, considering the flatulence of so many reputed writers in Latin American fiction" (Flores 116).

We may surmise that Flores identifies this "new phase," which has come to be termed *la nueva narrativa* or the new narrative, in contrast to the realism and "*costumbrismo*" that preceded it.[11] Such novels tended to focus on the specific and the regional as well as being strongly identified with individual national literatures. The new narrative, which reached its pinnacle in the Boom, was in part a reaction against these prevailing styles.[12] It could even be argued, as Doris Sommer has notably done in her introduction to *Foundational Fictions,* that the Boom authors, in rejecting their literary predecessors, were actually a logical product of that very tradition. One cannot, after all, mount a backlash against a nonexistent past. Even if some of the Boom writers saw themselves as inventing a tradition where there was none, they were not actually inscripting a blank page but rather writing over, and in some ways successfully covering up, pre-existing text.

The depiction of the Boom as a backlash against realism still provides an incomplete picture of its relation to a Latin American literary history.

Much of what is considered innovative in Boom texts is, as many critics have noted, "a continuation of an experimental tendency that had long been gathering force in Spanish-American narrative" (Lindstrom 142). The *Vanguardias* or avant-garde movements that flourished in Latin America in the early part of this century were bold experimentations in form and content, particularly in poetry but carried into prose, and could probably be said to have contained the seeds of what would later be identified as magical realism.

Theoretical debates are still raging regarding magical realism—its definition, its history, and its political implications.[13] What we can conclude with some degree of certainty is that the emergence of magical realism as a consciously adopted narrative strategy that gave impetus to the Boom is both a historically constructed phenomenon as well as a literary reaction to previous generations of writers. Roberto González Echevarría, in *Myth and Archive,* proposes a theory of magical realism as part of a progressive development of Latin American narrative. According to González Echevarría, Latin American narrative has paralleled and appropriated the hegemonic discourse of each epoch. Archival fictions, such as Carpentier's *Los pasos perdidos* [*The Lost Steps*] and *Cien años de soledad* [*One Hundred Years of Solitude*] retrace and incorporate all historical discourses, fictionalizing them so as to ultimately establish fiction as the hegemonic discourse of their time. This approach can be useful in establishing both a historical and literary context for what critics call magical realism, as it has been practiced by Latin American authors.[14]

Because many nonspecialists first became aware of Latin American literature through the Boom, and in fact remain aware of it solely through these novels, there has been a tendency to view them outside of their historical and literary context, as if they emerged from a vacuum. This has led, as mentioned earlier, to a perception of magical realism as paradigmatic. It has also led to critical practices that dislocate the texts, denying their "situatedness" at every level.

To some extent, Boom texts facilitate readings that isolate the texts from their specific political and historical contexts.[15] With the Boom phenomenon, Latin American narrative "began to speak an international language" (Donoso 10).[16] That is to say, through both form and content, these novels had great appeal to readers in metropolitan centers who could admire the highly crafted narrative structures, as well as their innovative and often self-reflexive perspectives on reality. For this reason, many critics have adopted a humanistic, universalizing approach. Donald Shaw, for example, has concluded that these novels demonstrated the abandonment in Latin America of the *"novela comprometida"* or politically committed novel, and the emergence of the *"novela metafísica"* or metaphysical novel (Shaw, "Concerning" 322).

Other critics, however, have pointed out that while the Boom could be read as detached from sociopolitical concerns, such practices nullify the fact that texts, literary or otherwise, are at once products of history in the broader sense as well as participants in ongoing sociopolitical debates. Gerald Martin's *Journey through the Labyrinth: Latin American Fiction in the Twentieth Century*, for example, locates Latin American literature, including the Boom novels, in a sociopolitical context and highlights politicized readings.

At the other end of the critical spectrum, in terms of degree of contextualization and engagement with specific political struggles, is Richard Watson's reading of *One Hundred Years of Solitude*. His reading proposes that the novel is, in form and content, one of self-negation where death and life are the same thing, nothing changes, and ultimately everything is irrelevant, meaningless.[17] According to Watson, the novel "is a pig's tail. I do not know if the same ambiguity hangs on a Spanish pig's behind, and I am not going to look it up. I hope you can go from tail to tale in Spanish, because if you cannot, then the English novel is that much better than the Spanish" (Watson 90). In these lines, Watson centers his interpretation on the play between tail and tale, which is inoperative in Spanish (*cola* and *cuento* or *relato*, respectively). Yet, he is unconcerned regarding whether the connection does or does not work in the original language, since the book he is discussing is *One Hundred Years of Solitude*, "a novel in English written by Gregory Rabassa based on a novel in Spanish by Gabriel García Márquez. This is not merely because I don't read Spanish, but also because this text exists as an object in itself that has been received as a novel in English by numerous ordinary readers, critics, and even scholars" (Watson 89).

Watson's point, namely that a translation of a text becomes a different text, authored by the translator, has been articulated by various critics working in translation theory.[18] A particularly poignant illustration of this position is Borges's story "Pierre Menard, autor del Quijote" ["Pierre Menard, Author of the Quixote"]. The story explores various approaches to translation, leading to an exact reproduction of the Quixote being received as an "original" work by Pierre Menard. Watson's evaluation regarding the English language novel being "that much better than the Spanish" even echoes the critics' position in Borges's story.

The obvious fact that Boom novels relied on translation to reach the international audience, which in turn defined the Boom as a phenomenon, is a key point. Emir Rodríguez Monegal asserts that although conditions paving the way for the Boom were well underway in Latin America prior to the works appearing in translation, it is only after they are made available in French and English that they gain the audience and market that Latin American narrative had never before experienced.[19] For Monegal, the "Boom in translation" begins with Borges sharing the first Premio Formentor with Samuel Beckett and consequently his *Ficciones* appearing in translation throughout Europe and the United States in 1961.[20] Thus, while Borges's writing actually predates the Boom, its availability in translation links his work temporally to the phenomenon.

It seems particularly appropriate that translation has played such an important role in the reception of Boom novels, given that the process of translation itself is a running subtext within many of them. This is especially true in *Cien años de soledad,* as generations of the Buendía family struggle to decipher, or translate, Melquíadez's text written in Sanskrit.[21] The preoccupation with translation is actually not surprising in light of the Boom novels' obsession with the writing and reading process. Since we can ascertain that reading—making meaning through a deciphering of codes—is a form of translation, then the inverse, that translation is a form of reading, must also be considered. Gregory Rabassa makes the observation that "translation is the closest reading one can possibly give a text" (Rabassa 6).

Reading a work in translation, then, is performing a reading of a reading. This shift to the twice removed facilitates Watson's exclusion of García Márquez's novel and its language from his discussion and interpretation of the English language version. It is also worth mentioning that the translators responsible for rendering most Boom novels in English, Gregory Rabassa and Edith Grossman, approach translation as reproducing the text as if it had been written in English.[22] As translators, they seek semantic and cultural equivalents recognizable to an English-speaking audience. This, too, facilitates the displacement of the text. Yet, by isolating García Márquez's novel from its linguistic context, readers such as Watson are also isolating it from the historical and literary conditions that produced it.

The removal of Boom novels from their language, Spanish, also erases the hierarchical relationship between languages in a U.S. context. As Arteaga elucidates, in this country, Spanish is the language of the poor, the foreign, the disempowered and as such has become established as a low-status language (Arteaga 14). The fact that novels such as *One Hundred Years of Solitude* circulate in English translation, furthermore seamless translation, which provides the illusion of the books always existing in the English language, removes them from associations with Spanish. This is a main point of difference between Latin American Boom novels and Latina/o literature.

While there exists a corpus of Spanish language work by Latina/o writers, most of the literature published after 1970 is written in English.[23] This is partly due to Latinos reaching higher levels of formal education, which is in English, and English becoming the dominant language for many; that is, the primary language of public expression. It is also partly reflective of a conscious choice made by writers to reach a broader audience.[24] Yet, much of Latina/o literature in English retains elements of Spanish. Sometimes bilingualism is represented through words, phrases, or entire passages in Spanish or Spanglish, as is the case with Rudolfo Anaya's *Bless Me, Ultima*, Judith Ortiz Cofer's *The Line of the Sun*, and Gloria Anzaldúa's *Borderlands/La Frontera*.[25]

Other times, the text is entirely monolingual but bears traces of bilingualism through syntactical choices, rhythms, or over-translation.[26] For example, in José Antonio Villareal's novel, *Pocho*, the father's dialogue reproduces the rhythm and diction of formal Spanish, although it is entirely in English. Alberto Ríos also makes use of Spanish language syntax, as in the lines, "Nothing is bigger in a small town than two people in love without the permission of everybody" (Ríos 187). The lines reflect the Spanish word order for "*sin el permiso de todos*," which typically would be "translated" as "without everyone's permission." The use of over-translation is subtle in the vignette "Salvador Late or Early" by Sandra Cisneros.[27] The title is a literal translation of the Spanish phrase "tarde o temprano." Rather than rendering the phrase through equivalent translation, which would be "sooner or later," Cisneros opts for over-translation which gives the phrase, in English, a broader interpretative field while adding layers of meaning for the bilingual reader.[28]

Roberto Fernández, in his novel *Raining Backwards*, pushes over-translation to its limits for satiric effect. The novel gives readers absurdities such as an announcement in the "English Supplement" to the newsletter of "the Municipality of One Hundred Fires in Exile." This is a literal translation of *El Municipio de Cienfuegos en el exilio.* Not only is Cienfuegos, a city in Cuba, over-translated as "One Hundred Fires," but the proximity of the words "in Exile" adds to the absurdity since in English it is unclear who or what is in exile. The bizarre newsletter informs its readers that one of the members will "undergo surgery to correct the waterfall in her left eye" (Fernández 33–34). The Spanish word for waterfall is *catarata,* which is also the word for cataract.

Thus, although we might intuit that texts by Latin American authors, originally written in Spanish and then translated to English, would be perceived as more "foreign" than those by Latinas and Latinos writing in English, the inverse is actually true. And this has had an influence on reception. Because Boom novels gained a broad monolingual audience in the states prior to there being a wide circulation of Latina/o texts in English, language expectations, based on reading Spanish texts in translation, have carried over to readings of Latina/o texts. The presence of Spanish in these works has subsequently led to either selective and incomplete readings that ignore the presence of Spanish, as is the case with the critical reception of *Borderlands* (analyzed below in chapter 4), or readings that interpret the presence of Spanish as disruptive, alienating, or "picturesque."

The language difference between Boom novels in translation and Latina/o texts in English also points to another difference between the two groups, that of socioeconomic class. Because the language(s) of Latinos in the United States functions as "an automatic signaling system second only to race in identifying targets for possible privilege or discrimination" (Deutsch quoted in Califa 321), and also as markers of class status, Latino discourse also functions as a class marker in literary texts. While the discipline of Literary Studies is currently engaged in an internal struggle to include class differences in its project on "diversity," there still exists a qualitative differentiation between "high culture" and all other forms of artistic expression. As a result, the privileging of cultural productions that express the values and aesthetics of a white, Eurocentric, middle- and upper-class hegemony remains.

To some degree, the existence of Boom texts in translation distances these texts from the intertwined association between language hierarchies and those of class. But this class difference is also in some respects present, in a different way, in Boom novels in Spanish. The writers categorized as being part of the Boom are all, not coincidentally, from middle class, professional, and privileged backgrounds. Not surprisingly, their concerns and agendas as artists and members of the intelligentsia reflect this positioning. Their use of Spanish, too, aligns them with the hegemonic. Latin American nations also have internal language hierarchies, with Spanish, and Portuguese in the case of Brazil, being the language of domination. Thus, within their own national histories and cultures, Boom writers are located within the ruling class. They are linguistically, economically, and culturally closer to the conquerors than they are to the conquered, even if Latin America as a region is marginalized in the global marketplace.

For Latina and Latino writers in the United States, the relationship between their language(s) and the hegemonic is different, as is, for many, their socioeconomic class background. Most Latino writers have ties to institutions of higher learning, as is discussed more fully in chapter 5. Many, however, come from working-class or migrant agricultural labor families.[29] Although critics such as Juan Bruce-Novoa assert that the generalization of class difference has obscured the existence of a Chicano and Latino middle class, the fact remains that much of Latino fiction is written by authors such as Tomás Rivera, Helena Maria Viramóntes, Gloria Anzaldúa, Ana Castillo, Sandra Cisneros, and Abraham Rodríguez Jr., who are the first generation in their families to break into the middle class, and their work reflects, through both language and content, a working-class perspective.

Gender also seems to play a role in the reception of Boom fiction. Women are most conspicuous in this phenomenon through their absence.[30] The various projects that undergird the works of Boom authors are primarily masculinist.[31] In Latina/o fiction, on the other hand, women writers have come to a place of relative prominence, even if this is a recent phenomenon.[32] Not surprisingly, these authors are quite outspoken on the issue of women's oppression under patriarchy, focusing on conditions for Latinas within their immediate culture and community as well as in the larger society. These writers are in the process of scripting a feminist critique, which Chicano Movement ideology suppressed in constructing an oppositional identity based on purely masculine terms.[33] While earlier Chicano texts, for example, embraced La Raza, as defined through a Chicano male subjectivity, Sandra Cisneros dedicates *The House on Mango Street* to "Las Mujeres."

Given the differences between Boom authors (such as Cortázar, García Márquez, Fuentes, and Vargas-Llosa) and Latina/o writers, as well as differences in the historical and material conditions under which both groups of texts are produced, it follows that their respective agendas and locations in relation to a cultural hegemony are also different. These differences in turn inform how narrative strategies such as those classified under magical realism are used and to what ends. Reader expectations, developed through ahistorical and decontextualized readings of Boom fiction, indiscriminately lump simplistic paradigms of magical realism together with moments of "magic" or narratives of the unexpected in Latina/o fiction. This effectively erases the "situatedness" of both groups.

Some Latina/o texts are presumed to fit in a Boom tradition, as defined by perceptions of the Boom as spontaneously emerging from a vacuum. These texts, then, are evaluated as failures or pale imitations, when they do not meet readers' expectations. Barbara Kingsolver's review of Ana Castillo's *So Far from God,* for example, portrays the novel as "a sort of Latin American 'lite'" (Christian 14). Kingsolver opines that Castillo's novel "distinguish[es] itself from its South American predecessors by its chatty, accessible *Norteño* language and relentless good humor. Give it to people who always wanted to read *One Hundred Years of Solitude* but couldn't quite get through it" (Kingsolver 1).

Other reviewers have proven less "generous" than Kingsolver. For example, Andrei Codrescu's review of *Raining Backwards* laments the novel's missed opportunity and concludes that it would have been a much better book if "the echoes of Gabriel García Márquez that run like a ritual motif through it had been made conscious and dealt with intelligently" (Codrescu 27). Ironically, Fernández's novel contains a dizzying amount of literary references, allusions, and inside jokes. This intertextuality is of course missed by Codrescu, who only recognized those echoes of García Márquez.

Fernández's appropriation of magical realist codes is deployed so as to make the irretrievable past in Cuba unreal, mythic, literally out of this world. As the aging Mirta tells the young Eloy, "In all the beaches in Cuba the sand was made out of grated silver, though in Varadero it was also mixed with diamond dust. . . . The sun rose in the North and set in the South" (Fernández 12–13). Mirta's words also echo the *crónicas* of discovery, which similarly told of riches and natural marvels. Even the disorientation in her assertion that the sun "rose in the North and set in the South" parallels Columbus's diary, which is filled with navigational errors rationalized by the wonders of the New World.

Allusion to and appropriation of the discourse of discovery is also a component of Carpentier's "*lo real maravilloso*" as well as Gonzalez Echevarría's study of Latin American narrative.[34] Yet Fernández transforms its use by distancing Mirta's hyperbolic narrative from "reality." In parodying magical realism, the novel also satirizes the Cuban exile community's reconstruction of the island as a paradise on earth with a knowing wink to the reader that such a place exists solely in idealized memory. That is, it exists only in the imaginary. Mirta's memories of Cuba cannot exist in the real world, as we can humorously see in her attempt to recreate Varadero in her bathtub with talcum powder, a fan, wallpaper, and tinted water.

Fernández's second novel after *Raining Backwards, Holy Radishes!,* provides direct commentary on magical realism, referencing García Márquez. In this novel, two women in Belle Glade, Florida, carry out an ill-fated scheme to make money by charging the public admission to see, among other fabricated wonders, a creature they term "The Flying Garcia." This creature, far from magical, is a mongrel dog with feathers and other discards from a butcher shop glued to it. To further cement the connection to García Márquez, The Flying Garcia, like the writer, is said to hail from Aracataca.

Judith Ortiz Cofer makes similar use of magical realist codes in her novel *The Line of the Sun.* As Karen Christian has pointed out, the passages that are set in Puerto Rico parody magical realism, co-opting Marquezian diction and style as in the line, "Ramona and Rafael were to be man and wife not a full year after they faced each other on Mamá Cielo's porch" (Cofer 83). Yet the narrative style changes as time shifts to the present and the setting is no longer Puerto Rico, but New York. The powerful spiritism that was not out of place in the island that "was too lush, too green, too hot" (161) has no place in "el building" on the mainland, as proven by the fire resulting from one of the ceremonies gone awry. As in Fernández's novel, there is strict distinction between the here, the now, the "real," and the nostalgia of another place, another time, another reality.

This is quite different from the use of magical realism in *One Hundred Years of Solitude,* which functions to create an entire fictional reality enclosed within the covers of the book. That is, in the world of the novel, these occurrences are intended to be taken at face value, inseparable and indistinguishable from the ordinary, which is at times narrated as the marvelous. Recall, for example, the opening lines of the novel in which Coronel Aureliano Buendía recalls seeing ice for the first time.

Some Latina/o texts, such as Rudolfo Anaya's *Bless Me, Ultima* and John Rechy's *The Miraculous Day of Amalia Gómez,* confuse readers familiar with Boom fiction. This occurs because they narrate "unreal" or "magical" events but do not incorporate the narrative strategies and codes of magical realism. In contrast to texts such as *One Hundred Years of Soli-*

tude wherein magical occurrences or those at least out of the ordinary, such as Remedios's ascension and the town priest's levitation after drinking hot chocolate, take place without further explanation, in Anaya's novel as in Rechy's, the miraculous occurrences are situated in specific cosmologies and carry spiritual dimensions different from those in Boom fiction. The Boom(ing) effect erases these differences, and in so doing reduces the complexity and heterogeneity of Latina/o conditions and struggles for representation to an identifiable and manageable "essence."

The Boom(ing) effect has also played a role in the marginalization of Latina/o literature within institutions of higher learning. Latina/o literatures' bilingualism—both the presence of Spanish in English language texts as well as its roots in Spanish language texts such as border ballads, poetry, and Spanish language journalism—is difficult to integrate into an English curriculum. Boom literature in translation is more easily "smuggled" across linguistic, class, and disciplinary borders, and the illusion of its emergence from nowhere alleviates the responsibility of contextualization.

The situation is no less conflicted in modern languages or Spanish departments. Here too, bilingualism plays a role, with the language(s) of Latinos, particularly variations of Spanglish, finding an unwelcoming reception. Course offerings on Latina/o literature are uneven, often taught, if at all, under special topics designations.[35] In many Spanish departments, Latina/o literatures are relegated to the status of "poor relations," or afterthoughts to Latin American literature, itself, until quite recently, the poor relation to Peninsular literature. Latina/o literature, then, is too often perceived as the poor relation to the poor relation, or second-generation illegitimate.

As institutions of higher learning struggle with curricular reform, and fields such as multiculturalism and cultural studies work toward canon revision and interdisciplinary methodologies, the role of the critic/teacher, too, is changing. As borders, be they geographic, political, socioeconomic, and disciplinary, become more and more porous, the critic/teacher's role becomes analogous to that of the coyote, a person who transports undocumented workers across the U.S./Mexico border for profit. Such an analogy may seem a bit forced and even insulting, given that the coyote is almost universally despised for reasons beyond the fact that her/his actions are illegal. Furthermore, comparing human lives—which are at stake daily in the dangerous literal border crossings—to texts may be interpreted as a form of denying the all too real conditions of those who undertake such journeys. Thus, it becomes imperative to specify that the analogy is posited with the intent that it lead to a more responsible and ethical scholarship and pedagogy as well as open up the potential of institutional reforms to bring about true change.

Identifying with the coyote means recognizing that as we introduce texts positioned either on or beyond disciplinary borders into circulation in the academic marketplace, we are engaged in a form of smuggling. Like the coyote, our position as go-between is conflicted in that we simultaneously function in the interest of our cargo as well as the interest of institutions of power, which on the one hand resist the newcomers while thriving on their potential for production.

As coyotes, we are also in positions of relative power since, as Rajeswari Mohan states, "whether texts serve an agenda of commodity fetishism or radical critique (these being but the two most compelling of any number of possibilities) would depend on the discourses which mediate them into the classroom" (Mohan 268). How we negotiate our role as mediators determines what type of coyote we choose to be. But no matter what our level of engagement, methodologies, ideologies, positionings, or other considerations that have a bearing on what and how we conduct scholarship as well as what and how we teach, we are in fact functioning as coyotes. To perform our jobs as both critics and teachers in an ethical, responsible manner we have to find ways to work within the coyote identity without reproducing the very hierarchical relations we seek to uncover and subvert; without, in other words, demanding too high a price for passage.

The coyote's job in transporting Latin American Boom fiction across national, linguistic, and disciplinary borders has proven to be too easy.[36] White, male, dressed in European clothes, and speaking through translation in unaccented English, these texts easily blend in. Without a past, their differences could be interpreted as exotic, the peculiar eccentricities of a well-traveled gentleman. For Latina/o texts, and in a different way for *testimonios*, the crossing has been more difficult. Their differences are self-consciously brought to the surface, a constant reminder of a past that goes unrecognized and a present filled with contradictions and fissures that resist resolutions. For coyotes engaged in this illicit, yet nonetheless necessary activity, the journey across the border is only part of our job. The other part, the more difficult one, necessitates a commitment—in our roles as teachers and scholars—to clearing and creating transformational spaces where these texts can refuse to blend in and instead engage with and revise their canonical and mainstream surroundings.

3

Out of Bounds

Testimonio and Its Reception

> They've always said, poor Indians they can't speak, so many speak for them. That's why I decided to learn Spanish.
>
> Rigoberta Menchú

> We want to be the voice of those who have no voice? An unfortunate expression. Well intentioned, but mistaken. There are no mute peoples. It is simply the case that the dominant culture, a culture of echoes of foreign voices, covers the mouths of those who have a voice of their own.
>
> Eduardo Galeano

The genre of *testimonio,* in spite of its claim to transparency and "reality," or perhaps because of it, poses challenges for the reader/critic. This form of expression, which on the surface appears to be straightforward, puts into question the very notions of genre, literature, historiography, and the relationship of all of these to political practices. That *testimonio,* as defined and discussed here, is a Third World cultural product, furthermore one that aims to provide the subaltern with a public voice, places critical inquiry on the genre and specific texts classified under it squarely in the terrain of asymmetrical exchanges (of goods, labor, capital, and culture) between the First and Third World. The reception of these texts within U.S. institutions, by necessity, becomes itself a field of inquiry. This inquiry can make explicit the implications of *testimonio*'s inclusion in and exclusion from academic discourses on race, class, gender, and transnational power structures.

John Beverley defines *testimonio* as

> a novel or novella-length narrative in book or pamphlet (that is, printed as opposed to acoustic) form, told in the first person by a

> narrator who is also the real protagonist or witness of the events he or she recounts, and whose unit of narration is usually a "life" or a significant life experience. *Testimonio* may include but is not subsumed under, any of the following textual categories, some of which are conventionally considered literature, others not: autobiography, autobiographical novel, oral history, memoir, confession, diary, interview, eyewitness report, life history, *novela-testimonio,* nonfiction novel, or "facto-graphic literature." (Beverley, "The Margin" 12–13)

In that article, Beverley goes on to further delineate what *testimonio* is, but only, as implied by the above quote, by explaining *what it is not.* That is, he discusses how it differs, in terms of production and effect, from those genres with which it occasionally overlaps. This process of definition by negation is most evident in descriptions of *testimonio*'s relation to two superficially dissimilar genres: autobiography and the novel.

Positing *testimonio* as an emerging genre in comparison to more established ones such as autobiography and the novel carries the risk of treating these genres as stable and uncontested; something that is simply untrue. What we may be able to agree upon is that these genres have been formulated and "tracked" in terms of conventions and development. Consequently, we have at our disposal a "grammar" from which we can speak about them and articulate arguments regarding a given text's place or lack of place in the canon. In the case of *testimonio,* texts have been produced and circulated, and even in certain cases been incorporated, however problematically, into existing literary structures, without the availability of such a "grammar." The critic then, at this moment, can only approach these texts indirectly, through borrowed language.

If we choose to approach *testimonio* through the borrowed language of autobiography, we must do so with full knowledge of what the term implies in theory and practice. Julia Watson and Sidonie Smith point out that "although the genres of life writing in the West emerge in Antiquity, the term *autobiography* is a post-Enlightenment coinage. Yet the word and the practice invoke a particular genealogy, resonant ideology, and discursive imperative" (Smith and Watson xvii). In his 1956 essay "Conditions and Limits of Autobiography," George Gusdorf attempts to fix the limits of autobiography and, not surprisingly, draws the boundaries around Western civilization in terms unambiguously male. He writes, "It would seem that autobiography is not to be found outside of our cultural area: one would say that it expresses a concern peculiar to Western man, a concern that has been of good use in his systematic conquest of the universe and that he has communicated to men of other cultures; but those men will thereby have been annexed by a sort of intellectual colonizing to a mentality that was not their own" (Gusdorf 29).

While Gusdorf's definition has gone through significant revisions in the past forty years, by critics as well as practitioners of autobiography, what remains a constant is the understanding that autobiography has participated in the cultural mythmaking of a specific kind of "selfhood," one in which "all 'I's' are rational, agentive, unitary, [and] all 'I's' are potentially interesting autobiographers . . . yet, not all are 'I's.' Where Western eyes see Man as a unique individual rather than a member of a collectivity, of race or nation, of sex or sexual preference, Western eyes see the colonized as amorphous generalized collectivity" (Smith and Watson xvii). To produce autobiographical texts, outside or on the margins of Western culture, is itself a transgression of the genre, one wrought with conflict given the problematic ideological assumptions embedded in the practice of autobiography.

Texts that transgress the limits of autobiography have been classified by Caren Kaplan as falling under the term "out-law" genres. She argues that such texts, including but not limited to *testimonios,* violate Derrida's definition of "The Law of Genre":

> As soon as the word "genre" is sounded, as soon as it is heard, as soon as one attempts to conceive it, a limit is drawn. And when a limit is established, norms and interdictions are not far behind. . . . Thus, as soon as genre announces itself, one must respect a norm, one must not cross a line of demarcation, one must not risk impurity, anomaly or monstrosity. (Derrida, "Genre" 203–4)

The status of *testimonio* as an "out-law" genre, and the problematic reception that such a status implies, can be analyzed in the critical responses to one specific *testimonio: I, Rigoberta Menchú, An Indian Woman in Guatemala* [*Me llamo Rigoberta Menchú y así me nació la consiencia*] by Rigoberta Menchú with Elisabeth Burgos Debray. This particular text is taken here as exemplary, but only with a certain degree of trepidation, since *testimonio,* as Beverley states in the disclaimer to his definition, "is by nature a protean and demotic form not yet subject to legislation by a normative literary establishment" (Beverley, "Margin" 93). To posit a certain text as "exemplary" is at least partially a move toward "standardizing" or "fixing" the genre so as to clear the way for smooth incorporation. It is, in other words, a strategy that carries the potential for neutralization.

Grounding this discussion on this particular text was rather a decision based on the existence of research, the availability of the text in English translation, and the inclusion of the text in courses outside of Spanish and Latin American Studies departments. *I, Rigoberta Menchú* is of particular importance in debates over curricular issues, since it is included on the reading list for one track of the humanities curriculum at Stanford University. It is thus exemplary, not in that it sets or enforces norms, but rather in that it can illuminate the dynamics of reception within U.S. institutions.

This particular *testimonio* is also useful in this discussion due to its more recent involvement in yet another controversy. In 1998, the U.S. anthropologist David Stoll published *Rigoberta Menchú and the History of All Poor Guatemalans,* which challenged the veracity of Menchú's story.[1] There followed a flurry of reports in the mainstream media as well as Menchú's response defending the core truth of her account as well as her right to tell her own story.[2] While controversy has died down, and the book continued to be taught in many university courses, Stoll's book and the ensuing debates highlight central issues that are relevant to the study of all *testimonios.*

The controversy brings to the surface questions on the very notion of "truth." Stoll's book casts doubt on certain points of Menchú's account based on contradictory statements from others. What it comes down to is that there are competing "truths" and each narrative presents its own version. In light of this, the discussion of this particular *testimonio,* or any other for that matter, goes well beyond the sorting of the "true" and the "false" and moves toward questions of representation and the construction of historical memory. Marc Zimmerman, writing years prior to the publication of Stoll's book, states that "whatever doubts have been raised about details of Rigoberta's story, they have failed to shake the foundations: the atrocities, the losses in the context of events that many people know of from a wide variety of printed and taped accounts" (Zimmerman 112).[3]

Issues of representation are bound up with another issue highlighted by the controversy surrounding Stoll's book—namely the question of who has the authority to represent "truth" and how. Because all events that we do not witness firsthand are available to us solely through competing narratives, the official or accepted version is constructed by institutionally sanctioned authorities. In this process, "testimonial narrators like Rigoberta Menchú [are granted] only the possibility of being witnesses, but not the power to create their own narrative authority and negotiate its conditions of truth and representativity (Beverley, "The Real Thing" 276).

Arturo Arias, writing specifically about Stoll's accusations against Menchú, ties together issues of "truth," "authenticity," and the Other's discursive authority. He writes, "We can only expect an absolute truth if we believe in perfectly verifiable truths or if we still see or insist on seeing 'authentic' indigenous subjects as noble savages whose alleged primitiveness puts them closer to some imagined natural truth. According to this criteria, indigenous persons who use discourse strategically either lose authenticity or are being manipulated by outside forces" (Arias 76).

What Arias points to is the lack of recognition of subaltern subjects as creators of their discourse, a critical resistance that lies at the center of the difficulty in approaching *testimonios.* This resistance to relinquishing our power of interpretation, experienced and explored by Behar in *Translated Woman,* is also at play, in a different way, in the reception of Gloria Anzaldúa's *Borderlands/La Frontera,* which is further discussed in chapter 4.

Yet a third issue brought out by the Stoll book controversy is the question of authorship. Because *I, Rigoberta Menchú* was actually organized and written by Elisabeth Burgos Debray, and in some editions it is Burgos who is listed as the author, questions of accuracy were compounded. This ambiguity in terms of authorship is a distinguishing characteristic of *testimonio.* It is a key element in Kaplan's definition of "out-law" genres. According to Kaplan, *testimonio* falls under the classification of "out-law genres" because it requires collaboration across participants' class and, often, racial differences. This process of collaboration, which violates the very notion of a singular and autonomous author, makes this text "impure," and arguably a "monstrosity," a deformation that makes the text at once an object of derision and dangerous. "Thus, instead of a discourse of individual authorship, we find a discourse of situation; a 'politics of location'" (Kaplan 119).

As a *testimonio* travels from the mouth of the testimonial subject or the "autobiolocutor," to the notes and tape recorder of the editor or transcriber, and then to the written form to be "cut, cut, and cut away," as Behar describes, to be transformed into a recognizable "book," mediation upon mediation takes place. These mediations are then compounded once the text is translated into English, a necessary process if it is to circulate outside of Spanish and Latin American Studies departments in U.S. institutions.[4] To ignore the role of the editor in the production of a *testimonio* becomes more than a question of irresponsibility. It becomes a form of recolonization by reproducing the dubious assumption that the "Other's" discourse can be rendered transparent and knowable in a decontextualized, ahistorical space where power hierarchies and positions of privilege and oppression either play no significant role or go unquestioned.

In the case of *I, Rigoberta Menchú,* the ten-page introduction by Elisabeth Burgos Debray reveals the pivotal role of the editor and the importance of scrutinizing the process behind the production of a *testimonio,* but it does so mostly by what it conceals. At the time of their meeting, Menchú was twenty-three years old, exiled from her native country of Guatemala for her activities as a revolutionary leader and participant in the guerrilla war of resistance. During the week that the two women spent together, in Burgos's Paris flat, Menchú recounted her life and described her traditions and customs as a Quiché. The original Spanish title, *Me llamo Rigoberta Menchú y así me nació la conciencia* [My name is Rigoberta Menchú and this is how I came to consciousness] is closer to the content of her story, which centers on her coming to political consciousness and action in the context of Guatemala's external and internal colonial history.

For readers, information as to what transpired during the time the two women spent together is available solely through Burgos's introduction, in which she relates and interprets specific moments of communication and exchange between herself and Menchú. This account has been closely analyzed by several critics as reproducing the very same structures that Menchú's story questions and resists. For example, Burgos denies Menchú's specificity and lapses into an essentialist description in referring to her skill in making *tortillas* as "a reflex thousands of years old," ignoring Menchú's accounts, which Burgos herself is editing, of the exploitation of this skill, which she learned from her mother, by the landowners as well as the urban middle class (Carr 84).

This representation of "the Other" as static, knowable, and ahistorical is also evident in the editor's description of her first impression of Menchú: "The first thing that struck me about her was her open, almost child-like smile. Her face was round and moon-shaped. Her expression was as guileless as that of a child and a smile hovered permanently on her lips" (Burgos Debray xiv). The language used here is a reproduction of the discourse of colonization, with its descriptions of "natives" as docile, ingenious children dependent on the colonizer.

Yet some critics seem to overlook this, taking Burgos's words as fact rather than interpretation. Rosemary Geisdorfer Feal in her article, "Spanish American Ethnobiography and the Slave Narrative Tradition," for example, first acknowledges the mediative function of the editor and dutifully notes, "Even transcripts of ethnographic interviews, such as those undertaken by Oscar Lewis, imply an ideological stance, a perspective, a selection of speaker and circumstance" (Geisdorfer Feal 103). Yet scarcely two paragraphs later, she treats Burgos's introduction as if it were authoritative and objective, introducing her citations of Burgos's text with the detached vocabulary of science: "as she reports . . ." (Geisdorfer Feal 103).

What Burgos, a white anthropologist from Venezuela, "reports" is summarized by Geisdorfer Feal in the following way:

> The two women share the same household for eight days; their relationship intensified when Menchú discovered that Burgos had a supply of maize flour and black beans, the staple diet in the Guatemalan highlands as well as in the Venezuelan culture in which Burgos grew up. In making and breaking tortillas together, these women solidified their part of the ethnobiographic pact. (Geisdorfer Feal 103)

What Geisdorfer Feal erases from Burgos's introduction is a reflection of what Burgos's own text occludes, namely that "breaking tortillas together" reproduces on several levels the historical power relations that account for the differences between the two women. The household the two women "share" is not the neutral space the word implies. It belongs to Burgos and Menchú is a visitor for the duration of the collaboration. Burgos's text performs this same type of erasure of the two women's differential relationship to the space they inhabit by stating that "For the whole of that week I lived in Rigoberta's world" (Burgos Debray xv), presumably meaning it metaphorically. In actuality the Paris flat was as far removed from Menchú's world as one could possibly get, and ownership or at least legitimate occupancy belonged solely to Burgos.

In order for the two women to "break tortillas" together, it is Menchú who does the cooking. Burgos writes,

> The first thing Rigoberta did when she got up in the morning was make dough and cook *tortillas* for breakfast; it was a reflex that was thousands of years old. She did the same at noon and in the evening. It was a pleasure to watch her. Within seconds, perfectly round, paper-thin *tortillas* would materialize in her hands, as though by miracle. The women I had watched in my childhood made *arepas* by patting the dough flat between the palms of their hands, but Rigoberta made

> her *tortillas* by patting it between her fingers. . . . "We only trust people who eat what we eat," she told me one day as she tried to explain the relationship between the guerrillas and the Indian communities. I suddenly realized that she had begun to trust me. A relationship based upon food proves that there are areas where Indians and non-Indians can meet and share things: the *tortillas* and black beans brought us together because they gave us the same pleasure and awakened the same drives in both of us. (Burgos Debray xv–xvi)

As Robert Carr has commented, on this particular passage, it is an attempt to obliterate differences, thereby "domesticating Rigoberta and radicalizing herself" (Carr 83). The term *domesticating* is particularly appropriate since Burgos is effectively recasting Menchú as a domestic, a role she played for several years in Guatemala City. Menchú, the object of the more privileged white woman's gaze, is grouped by association with the domestics of Burgos's childhood, these other women whom she watched patting dough. Interestingly enough, this very association between her own spectatorship of "Other" women's labor spurs Burgos's "fantasy of two women who operate as equals within an exchange" (Carr 83).

Through her introduction, Burgos seeks to neutralize Menchú, relocating her in the discourse on "the Other," so that she can effectively appropriate her and her story. As Elizabeth Meese observes, regarding the introduction, "Fundamental differences inhabit these positions, Paris and Guatemala, the one who cooks and the other who watches, the Latin American and the Quiché Indian woman. The 'theorist' mis(re)presents the differences; the 'activist' appropriates them" (Meese 102). This ten-page text, then, makes the construction of Menchú's text, through Burgos, highly problematic and one that must be read with caution.[5] The introduction also turns the relationship (or "non-relationship" as Meese calls it) between the two women back against the reader so that we also must question our own positionings in relation to both of these women and the text they collaboratively produce.

Robert Carr has argued that *testimonio* involves a speaker from an exploited and oppressed community who works alongside someone who has, or can have access to the means of production of a commodity that can be marketed. Such a text inevitably extracts an experience from the Third World for consumption in the First World. Thus, it is imperative to recognize that First World/Third World relations are also implicitly in the text of "subaltern subjectivity," constructed in and between these interventions (Carr 85).

As First World readers and consumers of a *testimonio*, then, we too are implicated. Our association with the university renders our position more intensely conflicted. As Beverley notes,

> Literature and the university (in the historically specific form each takes during and after the Renaissance) have been, appearances to the contrary, mutually dependent on each other and as such deeply implicated in the processes of state formation and colonial expansion that define early modern Europe. This legacy still marks each, making their interaction in contemporary processes of decolonization and postcoloniality at the same time both necessary and problematic. (Beverley, "Second Thoughts" 3)

Menchú's narrative itself draws our attention to our own conflicted positionings. Her statements, repeated throughout the text, demonstrate her need to conceal parts of her story, and parts of herself.[6] In chapter 3, for example, she tells Burgos, "I can't tell you what my *nahual* is because that is one of our secrets" (Menchú, *I, Rigoberta* 34). The final lines of the book, which we may by convention expect to be the most resonant, make no attempt to embrace us, or draw closure to this narrative, but rather reinforce distance and deliberately leave an empty space, the space of that which we can't know: "Nevertheless, I'm still keeping my Indian identity a secret. I'm still keeping secret what I think no-one should know. Not even anthropologists or intellectuals, no matter how many books they have, can find out our secrets" (Menchú, *I, Rigoberta* 247).

Doris Sommer has observed that "Menchú invites us to a tete-a-tete, not a heart to heart" (quoted in Meese 99). This is understandable since information can and, as Menchú's experience has painfully taught her, will be held against her. She cannot exclude intellectuals as potentially dangerous to herself and her *compañeros* since it is no mere coincidence that Latin American Studies programs experienced their most significant boom during the Reagan administration, which as Beverley points out, actually took Latin America seriously. While funding for such programs may have suffered in the 1980s, the work they produced was of interest to agencies seeking to protect "national security" and gather "intelligence" on the region.

It is absolutely clear that the speaker in *testimonio* is relating his or her story with the intent of bringing about specific material change, one based on politicizing the reader/consumer. In this regard it is what Barbara Harlow has termed "resistance literature." The efficacy of such a literature rests on its oppositional and revolutionary function, which ceases to function in that way once the text is assimilated by hegemonic institutions. Thus, in whose interest and to what ends do we as critics perform our rhetorical gymnastics attempting to "legitimize" the genre by reifying its literariness in First World terms, so that we can comfortably fit it into existing structures, leaving such structures intact? This slippery space is the contradictory and highly charged terrain where criticism of *testimonio* takes place.

As we engage with these texts, our own participation in global systems of economic exchange and exploitation and the ease with which we can reproduce these systems through our own scholarship and teaching must become a focal point of investigation and ongoing debate. Ironically, even *testimonio*'s most ardent supporters occasionally become trapped in the desire to legitimize these texts by arguing their "literariness" in terms that have become established in First World discourses. One such example is Beverley's assessment of Menchú's detailed description of her mother's and brother's torture and murder in the hands of the Guatemalan army as containing a "hallucinatory and symbolic intensity different from the matter-of-fact narration one expects from *testimonio*. One could say this is a kind of testimonial expressionism, or 'magical realism'" (Beverley, "The Margin" 101).

This appeal to literariness works against Beverley's principal intent in that article, namely to highlight the need to negotiate the differential relationship between reading Third World *testimonio* and reading "literature" in the First World. It is a form of what Mohanty has termed "discursive colonization." Ketu Katrak has described this phenomenon as "a Western theoretician's tendency, even with the best intentions and political sympathies, to appropriate 'third world' texts within an intellectual hegemony" (Katrak 160).[7] Carr insightfully notes that "we can learn much from Beverley's misconception regarding 'magical realism': in the process of configuring the space between *testimonio* and 'literature,' in broad terms, I would in contrast foreground the politicization of 'literature' rather than aestheticizing *testimonio*" (Carr 78).

Beverley reenters this critical dialogue with his essay, "'Through All Things Modern': Second Thoughts on *Testimonio*," which reframes the discussion of the genre in terms that are not in direct conflict with Carr's position but that nonetheless demonstrate the difficulty in articulating *testimonio*'s anti-literary function. Beverley argues that the aesthetics of *testimonio* are actually an anti-aesthetics, which makes the genre subversive in the context of literary studies. Yet in thus arguing he uses terminology, such as "defamiliarization," that has established itself as conventional in theorizing "literariness." Beverley writes,

> At least part of its aesthetic effect—I mean this precisely in the Russian Formalist sense of *ostrananie* or defamiliarization—is that it is not literary, not linguistically elaborated or authorial. . . . Even where its instrumentality is to reach in printed form a metropolitan reading public culturally and physically distant from the position and situation of its narrator, *testimonio* is not engendered out of the same humanist ideology of the literary that motivates its reception by this public or its incorporation into the humanities curriculum; and in some cases it actually resists being literature. (Beverley, "Second Thoughts" 8)

The opening lines of *I, Rigoberta Menchú* illustrate Beverley's point regarding *testimonio*'s resistance to being read as literature. "My name is Rigoberta Menchú. I am twenty-three years old. This is my testimony. I didn't learn it from a book, and I didn't learn it alone" (Menchú 1). The lines succinctly express the text's difference from and opposition to that which we conventionally identify as the literary. They subvert the autobiographical "I," which narrates experience and selfhood as differentiation from other "I's." In *I, Rigoberta Menchú*, the "I" moves in the opposite direction, toward the formation of a "we." The "I" functions throughout the text, not in an individualistic and autonomous mode, but rather as an "affirmation of the individual self in a collective mode" (Beverley, "The Margin" 17). Menchú goes on to state, "My personal experience is the reality of a whole people" (Menchú, *I, Rigoberta* 1). This key point in Menchú's narration is lost in the translation of the title from *Me llamo Rigoberta Menchú* to *I, Rigoberta Menchú* which is indicative of the cultural bias favoring singularity.

Fredric Jameson interprets Menchú's revision of the autobiographical "I" as a radical Third World decentering of the subject which enables us to break from the "authority" of the formerly unified subject/private property and bring about a new collective space between known subjects and individual human beings. This type of anonymity does not imply the loss of the proper name or personal identity, but rather its multiplication. He writes,

> Anonymity then, [expresses] . . . the relation of one individual to a plurality of other names and other concrete individuals. This is, then,

> a concept which is as much literary (having to do with the nature of a type of narrative discourse and its basic classification of the character, or more specifically the protagonist—the hero or heroine) as it is social, to the extent that it offers what I believe is a new conceptualization quite different from the menacing mob and the faceless masses of First World fantasies: a vision of collectivity and collective life specific to the culture and experience of the Third World itself. (Jameson 129)

Menchú's *testimonio* also engages in a revision of the novel, paralleling the ways in which all autobiographical narratives depart from, overlap with, and revise the genre. Many critics have argued that the distinction between fiction and nonfiction is illusory. E. L. Doctorow, for example, summarizes this position by saying, "there is no fiction or nonfiction as we commonly understand the distinction: there is only narrative" (Doctorow 231). From this statement we can extract the position that reality itself is a fiction, a text; and by extension, our only reality is fiction. Klinkowitz argues that "we know reality only through our fictions," and thus, "reminding readers that fictions are provisional realities and not bedrock truth is the essence of self-apparent writing" (Klinkowitz 135).

What is here referred to as "self-apparent writing" could be easily applied to the fiction of the Boom, with the novel *One Hundred Years of Solitude* as the most cited example. Roberto González Echevarría, in his influential study *Myth and Archive,* argues that Latin American narrative has followed a direct lineage paralleling and appropriating the hegemonic discourse of each particular period. This lineage culminates in the Boom fiction, which establishes fiction itself as the hegemonic discourse by retracing and fictionalizing all of the previous hegemonic discourses in "the Archive." What these novels do, then, is take the blurring of boundaries between fiction and nonfiction one step further and subsume nonfiction as a form under fiction.

Testimonio's relationship to the novels of the Boom is also evident in the emerging genre's history. In 1970, the Cuban publishing house Casa de las Américas began awarding a prize for *testimonio.* This decision was in part a reaction against the high aesthetics of Boom fiction, perceived by then to be antithetical to sociopolitical concerns.[8] While chapter 2 of this study discusses the relationship of the Boom to Latina/o literatures in the United States, a different relationship also exists between Boom novels and *testimonio.* This relationship is based on *testimonio* at times being promoted as the "authentic" form of Latin American, or even Third World, representation, in opposition to Boom fiction. Such a formulation falls prey to essentialist arguments that oversimplify both the Boom and *testimonio.* That is to say, situating *testimonio* in relation to the novel, and Boom novels in particular, is imperative, yet, in doing so, we must also be wary of relying on arguments of "authenticity."

Testimonio differentiates itself from the novel and the Latin American Boom novel in particular in that it "never puts the referentiality of language into question" (Sommer quoted in Meese 98). Moreover, it stands in sharp contrast to the texts examined by González Echevarría in that it posits experience and orality as more valid than theory and the written word. Whereas, in the Boom fictions, books and writing encompass all of reality—recall for example that the very existence of the town of Macondo was predicated on its being written in Malquíades's manuscript and once the manuscript is deciphered, the town literally blows away—in *testimonio* reality is constructed not only outside of writing, but in opposition to it.

Menchú's denial of an epistemology based on literacy transgresses humanistic ideology and articulates a theory outside of theory. It is useful here to situate her relationship to the written word in historical context, something Menchú herself provides for the reader in those passages describing her community's experiences with schools, teachers, and books. Her father's reasons for not sending his children to school align his decision with resistance to assimilation, which was, and still is, the goal of public education.

The relationship between writing and colonization in the Americas dates back to the fifteenth century and is evident in the *crónicas* written by the conquerors. As many critics, including Angel Rama in his now classic study *La ciudad letrada* [*The Lettered City*], have noted, throughout the colonial period, the printed word was used as both an instrument of domination, in terms of its legislative power, and in rhetorically constructing hierarchies that legitimated, consolidated, and propagated power. Five centuries later, Menchú's narrative demonstrates that present-day Guatemala is still struggling with this historical link between literacy and domination (Smorkaloff 103).

When in chapter 5 Menchú recounts her first visit to Guatemala City, it is the image of the typewriter that lingers in her mind:

> We went in and I saw my father take off his hat and give a sort of bow to the man sitting at a big table writing something on a typewriter. That's something else I used to dream about—that typewriter. How

> was it possible for paper to come out with things written on it? I didn't know what to think of all those people but I thought they were important people because my father took off his hat and spoke to them in a very humble way. . . . The city for me was a monster, something alien, different. . . . For me it was the world of the *ladinos.* (Menchú, *I, Rigoberta* 32)

In this passage, Menchú conflates the typewriter—an instrument of technology as well as one that stands for print culture—with intimidation and oppression.[9] It is the image of the city, the monster, which inhabits and stands in place of this space that is not hers, the seat of *ladino* power. In passages such as this, Menchú constructs the written word as an instrument of domination, the medium through which power hierarchies are established and reproduced. It is shown to be a marker separating those in power from the disempowered.

This construct is arguably embedded in the formation of genres such as autobiography and the novel. Yet, Menchú approaches it from a radically differently positioned perspective. Autobiography, for example, recognizes the power of the written word and appropriates it in the service of the autobiographical "I"'s self-formation. The novel also seizes the power of the written word and through it constructs an entire reality. In contrast to this, Menchú's narrative, spoken in a language not her own, and then ordered, written, and edited by someone unequivocally different from herself, can lay claim to being oppositional to the written word, even as it is paradoxically present to us solely in that form.

This paradox is at the center of what makes the entry and circulation of this text in the U.S. academic marketplace a conflicted process. It challenges our entrenched notions of the literary, as well as our established reading conventions, which have developed over time in conjunction with and in response to assumptions regarding literacy and its role in the struggle to obtain and/or propagate the distribution of power.

I, Rigoberta Menchú, like other *testimonios,* complicates the dialogic relationship between text and reader, subverting and problematizing the underlying set of assumptions we as readers rely on in making meaning as we engage with the text. This relationship is dialogic based on both the text's ongoing dialogue with other texts, which may or may not exist in written form, as well as the reader's expectations based on prior knowledge. In the case of *testimonio,* the collaborative process behind its production renders its dialogic engagement with other texts, that is, its intertextuality, multiply directed and even internally dialogic.

Menchú's oral narrative is uttered in a specific context of speaker and listener, as well as being located in and constructed in relation to oral traditions, cultural expressions, customs, conventions, and even grammatical structures not available to us as readers of the text. This is partly the result of Menchú's own process of concealment but also a built-in characteristic of the genre, which is heavily mediated. Superimposed on this narrative is Burgos Debray's manipulation of the oral narrative and her written text's location in relation to a different set of texts and conventions. *I, Rigoberta Menchú* is also engaged in an internal dialogue between Menchú's narrative and that of Burgos Debray.

Dialogic relationships have been articulated and explored by Bakhtin, particularly in relation to the novel. He argues for that genre's heteroglossia, wherein various differently positioned discourses are simultaneously presented. Yet, *testimonio* defies being subsumed under the parameters of that genre. It differs particularly in its mode of production as well as its primary intent, which is to inform and mobilize the reader to political action. While individual *testimonios* may gain and attain a "cultural value" that will secure their place in literary history far into the future, their primary intent is strictly pragmatic. *Testimonio*'s language and direct style also stand in contrast to those of the novel. While it may hold that truth is at times stranger than fiction, as it is narrated, truth is structured differently. To attempt to read it as fiction can, and in the case of *testimonio* often does, leave the reader frustrated and disillusioned. To put it more bluntly, *testimonios* make bad novels.

At the moment the reader engages with the text, there emerges yet another dialogic relationship consisting of the reader's dialogue with the text, not as a passive blank slate but as an active participant employing various reading strategies and critical conventions. To make meaning, the reader must not only decipher encoded words but textual codes as well, codes that presume the reader's and the text's interpretive community to be determined by acculturation in a Western culture of literacy. Even Shklovsky's conceptualization of defamiliarization assumes a shared understanding of what we mean by the familiar. Beverley's assertion of *testimonio*'s use of defamiliarization is for this reason invalid. If in fact *testimonio* presents the familiar in a manner that the reader can identify as different from other genres and texts, it is not because it makes use of literary artifice, but rather because the very notion of the familiar is inoperative. It is here that *testimonio*'s power, and some would say danger, lies.

Testimonio frustrates our desire to make meaning through reading strategies informed by a culture of literacy and an epistemology rooted in that culture. As readers and critics we are further frustrated by an inability to articulate a critical discourse on the genre. *Testimonio* resists the borrowed language of autobiography with its emphasis on the "I," as well as the borrowed language of the novel, a Western form that emphasizes in structure and narration the formulation of an imaginary reality. To read *testimonio,* then, requires that we develop new and specific reading strategies. This implies not only a revision of established strategies, but a questioning of these strategies as well as a problematizing of the political implications of employing critical conventions. It also necessitates a questioning of our complicity in colonizing practices as we engage with Third World cultural productions through these strategies and conventions.

It may be easy to classify *testimonio* as a border crosser; yet, it may be more fruitful to approach these texts as border dwellers. *Testimonio* bridges the space between the oral and the written by presenting itself in written form but referring back to a moment of speech. It is also evident that it is a physical border crosser in that it is intended to take a story from one geopolitical sphere to another. That is, *testimonio*'s intended audience is far removed in every imaginable way from the geographic area that contextualizes the interlocutor's account. Based on a marginalized subject's experience and shaped specifically for export to a metropolitan center, *testimonio* undoubtedly crosses borders. Yet, there is still the possibility of viewing these texts also as border dwellers.

Take, for example, after intense scholarly inquiry and debate, *testimonio*'s apparently permanent residence regarding its location in relation to the literary. It is not entirely "here" in the realm of what we traditionally term "literary" discourse. Nor is it entirely "there," floating ambiguously outside those limits where, for lack of a better term, all other forms of discourse reside. It is this resistance to standing squarely in any definable space that makes our task so daunting. As readers, critics, and teachers, we struggle to pull it away from those borders. Some achieve this by advocating the genre's citizenship in the literary landscape by arguing its literary elements or simply redrawing the border so as to relocate *testimonio* clearly within boundaries. Others attempt to fortify and make borders impenetrable so as to decidedly exclude *testimonio* from contact with the documented, established citizenry of Literary Studies. For the most part, critics working on *testimonio* have fallen into the first category and it is their work that has made these texts a subject of scholarship and required reading for legions of courses. In this respect, these critics/teachers have functioned as coyotes in the best sense of the word. They have brought these texts into academic discourse and, no doubt, inspired divergent modes of questioning not only in their fellow scholars but in their students as well.

As scholars and teachers, we continue to be challenged by *testimonio* to resist easy incorporation, which neutralizes the genre's revolutionary intent. In other words, assimilating the genre should not be our goal. To include a text such as *I, Rigoberta Menchú* on a syllabus is not in and of itself practicing diversity or employing a global approach. If the text is merely "tacked on," without teachers and students engaging in relational readings and pedagogy—that is, without allowing for the reading of *testimonio* to influence our reading of canonical texts—we are reproducing the very structures of differential power relations that Menchú's narrative critiques. To be truly inclusive in our scholarship and pedagogical practices, we must go well beyond the mere addition and instead utilize our reading of *testimonios* such as *I, Rigoberta Menchú* to clear a transformational space.

"Transformational" is used here in reference to changes in the individual reader as well as institutional structures. *Testimonio*'s potential lies in its ability to affect change in the individual reader in terms of her/his reading strategies as well as effecting a change in direct political action through solidarity with revolutionary struggles of liberation.[10] At the institutional level, *testimonio* puts into question entrenched notions of authorship, genre, and individual autonomy. *Testimonio* promotes a rethinking of categories such as knowledge, literature, theory, and reading as well as fostering an exploration of how these categories are constructed. Such a rethinking can produce a destabilizing effect on institutional structures that regulate access to power and its distribution.

To engage in transformational scholarship and teaching through *testimonio* means to subvert the established practice of reading marginalized texts through the strategies and conventions of the center and work toward re-reading the center through the marginalized. This transformational approach is a goal that has not been reached but that holds the promise of a truly inclusive and revisionist model that successfully negotiates the conflict between silencing and erasure on the one hand and appropriation and neutralization on the other.

4

Spic Spanglish?

The Reception of *Borderlands/La Frontera* and Linguistic Resistance

So, if you want to really hurt me, talk badly about my language. Ethnic identity is twin skin to linguistic identity—I am my language.

Gloria Anzaldúa, *Borderlands/La Frontera*

The struggle for Latina/o self-identity and self-representation is most passionately staged in the terrain of language(s). This struggle is both internal and external. It splits the multiple selves within the individual and divides various Latina/o groups from one another. Language use is also a marker of difference against U.S. hegemony. Unlike other groups, which Latinos are often compared to and pressured to emulate, Latinos have more intensely retained their language than any other group in history, with 90 percent of U.S. Latinos identifying themselves as Spanish speakers.[1] Linguistic affirmation, for many Latinas/os, is a strategy for "fending off a schizophrenia . . . that pathological duality born of contending cultural worlds and, perhaps more significantly, of conflicting pressures toward both exclusion and forced incorporation" (Flores and Yúdice 60).

Gloria Anzaldúa takes up the issue of language as a site of struggle in *Borderlands/La Frontera: The New Mestiza* by placing it, in terms of both form and content, at the center of her snakelike autobiographical narrative constructing a "New Mestiza consciousness." The reception of this text in the academy, however, is multilayered, and its inclusion in a broad range of courses transgresses disciplinary boundaries. This reflects the text's own scripting of border and mestiza consciousness. The book's structure, divided into two sections that interweave genres, is itself transgressive.[2] The first section, "Atravesando Fronteras/Crossing Borders," consists of seven autobiographical essays theorizing "the New Mestiza." The second section, "Un Agitado Viento/Ethécatl, the Wind" is composed of poetry. *Bor-*

derlands' problematic reception is also reflective of institutional conflicts, which are often resolved through the employment of various strategies of containment.

These strategies manifest themselves through instances of decontextualization—removing the text entirely from its geographic, historical, and cultural specificity. This decontextualization neutralizes the text and paves the way for appropriation. Another strategy of containment is the isolation of the text, the encapsulation of its discourse as entirely separate from competing discourses. This second strategy, like other strategies of containment, leaves the very structures of exclusion intact while providing the semblance of inclusion. It is, in practice, a form of the "tacking on syndrome" whereby the text is prevented from entering into dialogue with other, differently positioned texts. For example, rarely is the text read in dialogue or in conflict with other texts of feminist theory.

Whatever form these strategies of containment take, to be effective, that is, to present themselves as coherent, they ignore the role language plays in Anzaldúa's text. This omission is so pervasive that it begs the question: What is it about *Borderlands/La Frontera* and its languages that is so threatening that it must be ignored? The text itself is blatant about its concern with language struggle and resistance. It dedicates an entire chapter—"How to Tame a Wild Tongue"—to this very issue. Language struggle is even the medium itself, since the text uses several languages and does not always provide either direct or contextual translations. To begin to posit answers to this question of omission, or to even legitimate the question as such, we must first situate *Borderlands* and its languages within a historical, cultural, and critical context. In mapping out this context, rather than following tidy sections and chronological order, this chapter follows Anzaldúa's lead and unwinds itself—or winds itself—in a coiling structure, since all of these categories exist simultaneously and are embedded in one another.

In recent years, the drive to regulate minority discursive practices, particularly those of Latinas/os, is not only prevalent but actually increasing. This type of political and legal rhetoric functions to maintain U.S. cultural hegemony, or at least the illusion of it. Twenty-two states have passed legislation and even amended their state constitutions to become officially "English only." In 1993 alone, four bills were introduced in Congress to make English the national language (Arteaga 12). The prevailing argument, by which many Latinos and Latinas have been persuaded to vote in favor of these referendums, is that English-only legislation is purely "symbolic" and in practice does not discriminate against non–English speakers. Furthermore, according to this argument, bilingual Latinos are untouched by such measures.

Yet, if we unpack the rhetoric behind the English only movement, we can see that the "symbolism" of these laws and amendments is rooted in racism and in fact intended to have very real consequences in the material world.[3] Take, for example, the words of Terry Robbins, a former head of U.S. English operations in Florida:

> There are misguided persons, specifically Hispanic immigrants, who have chosen to come here and enjoy our freedoms, who would legislate another language, Spanish, as co-equal and co-legal with English. . . . If Hispanics get their way, perhaps someday Spanish could replace English entirely. . . . we ought to remind them, and better still educate them to the fact that the United States is not a mongrel nation. (Robbins quoted in Califa 321)

If these words seem to represent an extremist position, one that would hold no currency in academic circles, let us point out that the quote is taken from a speech delivered at Florida International University, whose student population is overwhelmingly Latino.

Robbins's equating of the term *Hispanic* with *immigrant* denies history, particularly of the Southwest, and works on the presumption of English as the pre-existing language. In this swift rhetorical move, Robbins erases the previous presence of Native American languages throughout the territory that presently comprises the United States, as well as the presence of Spanish, and in some areas, French as the first European languages to stamp themselves on this map. In what is now the Southwest, Spanish was the legal and national language until the signing of the Treaty of Guadalupe-Hidalgo in 1848, even if an overwhelming number of Anglo immigrants within this Mexican territory refused to speak it and tenaciously held on to English. As Alfred Arteaga summarizes:

> In order to foster an image of an America born in the English language, it becomes necessary to propagate a story of contiguous and historically English presence . . . [and this is accomplished by writing history] not chronologically but, rather, from East to West so that Spanish is encountered by the likes of Austin and Fremont during the Western expansion late in U.S. history; it appears *historically* after English. (Arteaga 25)

Robbins's use of the terms *co-equal* and *co-legal,* as offensive as they may be in the context of his argument, are actually quite accurate. There are those, as Robbins asserts, who struggle to make Spanish, and other languages and discursive practices such as Caló, co-equal and co-legal, but this struggle does not take place in the realm of legislation. For it to do so would imply a high level of power, one restricted at the present time to white and predominantly male members of this society. The struggle to assert linguistic equality takes place rather in the deployment of language in everyday life. It is on this terrain "that Latinos wage their cultural politics as a 'social movement'" (Flores and Yudíce 61).

A poignant example of this, and one that also illuminates the centrality of language as a site of resistance in Anzaldúa, is a political cartoon by Alejandro Sánchez, drawn in response to the 1994 Supreme Court decision that upheld a ruling in nine states allowing employers to prohibit workers from speaking any language other than English during working hours. The initial frame shows the seven judges who voted in favor of the ruling pointing large and accusing fingers—angry, scowling versions of the classic Uncle Sam pose. The second frame shows the decision in practice as two supervisors order two Latino workers to "speak only in English." In the next frame the workers respond "Sí se puede" [Yes, it can be done], to which one supervisor responds, "They're speaking in Spanish!" The workers continue to resist, bringing on a list of accusations and further restrictions: "They're whispering in Spanish! . . . They're lip-reading in Spanish! . . . They're writing notes in Spanish! . . . They're dressing in Spanish! . . . They're pronouncing city names [which are in Spanish] with a Spanish accent! . . . They're pronouncing their names with a Spanish accent!" Finally, "Their body language is in Spanish!" The final frame reads, "And thus, the R-R-Resistencia continues . . ." (A. Sánchez 36).

The humor in this cartoon is double-edged. On the one hand it demonstrates the absurdity of the ruling through the energy the supervisors must expend in enforcing it. The other side of this is that the supervisors are right on one key point and that is that language manifests itself through expression beyond utterance. Thus, language legislation, the codified form through which law reinforces the unequal relationship between English and Spanish, is also a way of legislating expression in the broader sense—the performance of identity, and even the physical manifestation of the self through the body. Of course the cartoon also demonstrates that linguistic resistance takes many forms. To put it another way, linguistic resistance is an observable form of political resistance that, given the current distribution of power, relies on alternative means of expression, that is, those not codified through law and other institutions of power.

While identity and transformational meaning are constructed and

Alejandro Sánchez, 1995. By permission of Arte Publico Press, University of Houston.

played out by both linguistic and paralinguistic means, language choices, syntax, and interlingual as well as intralingual communication are the most consistent and most obvious sites of self-representation and self-formation. Flores and Yudíce state:

> Language, then, is the necessary terrain on which Latinos negotiate value and attempt to reshape the institutions through which it is distributed. This is not to say that Latino identity is reduced to its linguistic dimensions. Rather, in the current sociopolitical structure of the United States, such matters rooted in the "private sphere," like language (for Latinos and other minorities), sexuality, body, and family definition (for women and gays and lesbians), etc., become the semiotic material around which identity is deployed in the "public sphere." (Flores and Yudíce 61)

Borderlands/La Frontera is a text that disrupts the hierarchies established to maintain the boundaries between the "private" and the "public" by incorporating and politicizing "matters rooted in the 'private sphere' like language . . . sexuality, body, and family definition." What Anzaldúa does, however, is doubly disruptive in that she also brings her Lesbian Self and her Chicana Self into polyglot dialogue. If as critics and teachers we ignore the role of language choice or, as Arteaga refers to it, "the form of the form," then we are only privy to a fraction of the conversation.

Arteaga, incorporating previous work on Chicano discourse by critics such as Rosaura Sánchez, argues that Chicano writing opposes the monologic discourse of U.S. American culture through the use of dialogic discursive practices.[4] If we know that language stratification and suppression has led to language becoming "an automatic signaling system second only to race in identifying targets for possible privilege or discrimination" (Deutsch quoted in Califa), and that "for Chicanos [and Puerto Ricans], linguistic practice has been the legal criteria to classify, to differentiate: Spanish Speaking, Spanish Surnamed, White Hispanic" (Arteaga 13), then we can accept Arteaga's argument that "Chicano subjectification is never far from the competition among languages" (Arteaga 13).

Anzaldúa's text demonstrates this, yet it strives to eliminate the term *competition,* at least as it applies to the internal struggle over language and how through language a "New Mestiza consciousness" is written into being. In her poem "To live in the Borderlands means you," the first stanza reads:

> are neither *hispana india negra española*
> *ni gabacha, eres mestiza,* mulata, half-breed
> caught in the crossfire between camps
> while carrying all five races on your back
> not knowing which side to turn to, run from.

The lines deny purity in any form, including linguistic purity, and assert hybridity, with the knowledge that the hybrid space is not the same as reconciliation, nor is it a place of safety. The final stanza of the poem declares:

> To survive the Borderlands
> you must live *sin fronteras*
> be a crossroads. (Anzaldúa 195)

Survival, then, is linked not to the resolution of dualities or conflicting identities, but rather to the ability to maintain conflict and difference without the defeat of one element over the other, that is, without resolution.

Anzaldúa's discourse—which points to multiple intersections of race, class, gender, sexuality, and language—reflects the complexity of representation as well as the conflicts and ambiguities that necessitate negotiations in everyday life. She discursively struggles to formulate an identity that does not reduce any aspect to a simplistic either/or paradigm. This includes her discourse on sexuality, which demonstrates Eve Sedgwick's assertion that heterosexist assumption organizes difference and conflict into a seamless and univocal whole around "sexual identity." In opposition to this, according to Sedgwick, "'Queer' can refer to: the open mesh of possibilities, gaps, overlaps, dissonances and resonances, lapses and excesses of meaning when the constituent elements of anyone's gender, of anyone's sexuality aren't made (or *can't be* made) to signify monolithically" (Sedgwick 8).

Chicana/o theorists, critics, and writers have similarly been challenging paradigms that promote monolithic representations of categories that limit the construction of meaning to either/or formulations. Refuting a conceptual map of the United States delineated by borders, Chicanas and Chicanos have been redrawing it as a cartography that is all border (Flores and Yudíce).[5] This paradigm, rather than facilitating co-optation and universalization, works toward an engagement that is relational and grounded in the specificities of difference. The conceptualized borderlands counter illusions of homogeneity. They contest hierarchical power relations by casting all modalities of differentiation as fluid and subject to continual negotiation and renegotiation without the necessity of resolution.

Mary Louise Pratt uses the phrase "criticism in the contact zone" to refer to theoretical constructs that posit ethnic cultures "as borderlands, sites of ongoing critical and inventive interaction with the dominant culture, as permeable contact zones across which significations move in many directions" (Pratt, "Criticism" 89). While Pratt argues for a "contact zone perspective" or "relational optic" in approaching cultural productions termed transnational or even postnational, she credits Chicano/a critics as leaders in this mode of inquiry. In stating, "That this perspective has been developed by Chicano/a cultural critics and theorists for whom the border exists not as a line but as an absolutely distinctive cultural space is no accident" (90). Pratt further grounds this (re)visioning in specifics of Chicana/o conditions.

Anzaldúa's text speaks from a multiplicity of borderlands, or rather takes the specific location of the border between Mexico and the states and naturalizes it as a cultural space that proposes a way of being with its own strategies for survival, representation, and self-creation. In positing the border as something other than the neat and tidy demarcation of the margin, the text pushes boundaries on all sides so that we can imagine various possibilities as coexisting. The text applies this to several categories of differentiation traditionally broken down in accordance with binary oppositions, such as Spanish/English, female/male, Mexico/United States, and so on.

Not surprisingly, then, Anzaldúa's use of the word *mestiza* is also positioned in the interstice of conflicting dualities. The word refers, in the literal sense, to the hybrid of Spanish and indigenous blood, as well as that of African slaves brought to the Americas following the conquest. The word is used by Anzaldúa in theorizing multiply embodied subjectivities, which places this text within a critical tradition that dates back to the nineteenth century in the Pan-American discourse of José Martí and the discourse on *mexicanidad* of José Vasconcelos. It also participates in dialogue with more recent theories of hybridity formulated by Chicanos and Chicanas. Thus, Anzaldúa's text does not exist in a critical vacuum, and reading it outside of this context can, and often does, lead to the "temptation to pedestalize or even fetishize *Borderlands* as the work of one unique individual" (Yarbro-Bejarano 8).

Part of Anzaldúa's critical context is situated on the other side of the border, which for many critics translates to that which is beyond the border, out of bounds. Yet, because Anzaldúa positions herself along a specific geographic border, which she describes as "*una herida abierta* where the Third World grates against the First and bleeds," it seems not only justifiable but necessary to extend her critical context outward toward Latin America.

The use of the word *mestiza* has deep roots in Latin American identity formation. José Martí, for example, in his essay "Nuestra América," refers to Latin America—which he defines as "our America" as opposed to the United States which he terms "the America which is not ours"—as "*nuestra América mestiza.*" Martí's project is defined as Pan-American since it strove to unite the newly independent nations of Latin America. The essay calls for resistance to both the cultural imperialism of European centers, specifically Paris, as well as the economic neocolonialism of the United States. Several critics, such as José David Saldívar, have extended the category of *nuestra America* to include racial and "conquered" minorities living within U.S. borders.[6] Anzaldúa's text makes further revisions to Martí's version of *mestizaje.* While Martí's essay was, and still is, in many ways radical, it established an ideological basis for differentiation from both Europe and the United States on purely masculine terms and left pre-independence racial and class structures unquestioned. Anzaldúa's use of the term *mestiza* implies a gendered subject and examines *mestizaje* as the struggle in and between languages, class, race, and sexualities.

A second text, from beyond the border, which also demands to be read as part of Anzaldúa's critical context is José Vasconcélos's *La raza cósmica* [*The Cosmic Race*], which has been influential not only in ongoing articulations of *mexicanidad* but in the Chicano Movement as well. Vasconcélos's theory of *mestizaje* centers on synthesis and is in effect a celebration of hybridity in racial and cultural terms.[7] The book became a central text for Chicano affirmation and it is from this text that the term *La raza* is reterritorialized. The centrality of this text, which proposed a mythology of Mexican *mestizaje,* is particularly evident in Anzaldúa's reconstruction of myth and history. Vasconcélos's presence in *Borderlands* is perhaps too obvious for Chicana/o critics to mention, but because *Borderlands* has itself become a border crosser, transgressing disciplinary boundaries, it is important to point out this connection so as to situate the text in a tradition of theorizing *mestizaje.*

Chicana feminist critics have been articulating gendered theories of multiply embodied subjectivities since the 1970s.[8] To a great extent, Chicanas' constructions of complex identities—that could incorporate, for example, gender, race, class, sexuality, and other factors—was a response to the Chicano Movement. Although it made great contributions to Chicana/o politics, art, and thought, the Movement promoted an ideology that constructed Chicano nationalism and Chicano identity in unambiguously, and exclusionary, male terms. This ideology in turn set up a false dichotomy whereby Chicanas either adopted the Chicano male identity or took on the role left to them: that of the victim and traitor personified by La Malinche (Chabram-Dernersesian, Yarbro-Bejarano).

Critics such as Angie Chabram-Dernersesian have taken on the role of historian, documenting the contributions that Chicana feminists made in the 1970s toward theories of multiple subjectivities. Chela Sandoval in the early 1980s called for models that could account for gender and sexualities in Chicana subjectivity. And Guillermo Gomez-Peña with the Border Arts Workshop and the publication of the journal *La linea quebrada/The Broken Line* in the mid-1980s has also been active and influential in generating dialogue within and about "borderness." Anzaldúa's *Borderlands* has firm roots in this intellectual community and tradition as is evident in her use of the term *New Mestiza* which implies prior formulations and models.

Through its deployment of languages, *Borderlands* carries *mestizaje* over into the linguistic realm and makes the reading process itself one of negotiating conflicting dualities, deciphering multiple sets of codes, and constantly (depending on readers' proficiency in these languages) engaging in the process of translation. The use of language, the "form of the form," is not solely the medium, but the message itself. To suppress the role language plays in this text is to deny engagement with the text and reduce "The New Mestiza" to a formulation that lies outside of the material world. The denial of language in *Borderlands* renders it an inert document, open to a process of dissection that can make of it nothing or anything at all.

The reception of *Borderlands* has, for the most part, severed the text from its critical context as well as from its language, and this has opened the door for readings that perceive it to be propagating essentialism or exceptionalism. At the other extreme, decontextualized readings have led to the universalizing of terms and experiences. A contextualized reading that situates the text in an ongoing tradition, carried out by Latin American and Chicana/o intellectuals theorizing *mestizaje*, can counter the drive toward exceptionalism. It can provide insight for critics and readers who, finding themselves disoriented by the so-called newness or alienness of the text, may resort to imposing paradigms and expectations that more closely fit critical traditions and strategies that are more familiar.

A case in point is a review essay that appeared in *Feminist Studies*. In this essay, Regenia Gagnier compares nine "feminist autobiographies" by African American, Jewish American, and Chicana authors.[9] Because Gagnier approaches these texts from a poststructuralist feminist perspective and situates them solely in that framework, she reads Anzaldúa narrowly through preferred reading conventions and chastises her for "still cling[ing] to more traditional, even romantic, conceptions of the artist and the self" (Gagnier 147).

Gagnier interprets Anzaldúa's conceptualization of the Self, and more specifically the writing Self, as "romantic individualism." According to Gagnier, "Anzaldúa suggests that women of color cling to the self because of their alienation from the mother culture and their alien status in the dominant culture" (Gagnier 140). The wording here implies a paraphrase of Anzaldúa, when in fact it is an interpretation. Gagnier's summation presumably is based on the following lines from *Borderlands:* "Alienated from her mother culture, 'alien' in the dominant culture, the woman of color does not feel safe within the inner life of her Self. Petrified, she can't respond, her face caught between *los intersticios,* the spaces between the different worlds she inhabits" (Anzaldúa 20). These lines imply, not a clinging to the self, which is described as a place of danger, but rather a different conceptualization of the self through what Anzaldúa terms "la facultad."

Empowered by the "New Mestiza consciousness," Anzaldúa can construct a self from "los interticios." She writes:

> What I want is an accounting with all three cultures—white, Mexican, Indian. I want the freedom to carve and chisel my own face, to staunch the bleeding with the ashes, to fashion my own gods out of my entrails. And if going home is denied me then I will have to stand and claim my space, making a new culture—*una cultura mestiza*—with my own lumber, my own bricks and mortar and my own feminist architecture. (Anzaldúa 22)

In *Borderlands,* the "lumber . . . bricks and mortar" are words which, formerly used against her to disempower, to marginalize, and to wound, are now being used to build, with Anzaldúa as architect, builder, and author.

In contrast to this, Gagnier "translates" her own reading of *Borderlands* into the following: "In literary critical terms, women who have never possessed the authorial signature are not ready to give themselves over to the deconstructive or postmodern 'death of the author,' and they cling more tenaciously to individualism" (Gagnier 140). Determined to approach feminist autobiography by women of color from the reductive perspective of the degree to which these texts subvert "their artistic brothers' pursuit of autonomy" (Gagnier 140) and conform to a monolithic notion of "the death of the author," the reviewer must then deny the texts' specific contexts. She must also deny the ways these texts may be commenting on these critical paradigms, but in ways that demand a greater degree of complexity in interpretative strategies on the part of the critic.

Doris Sommer, writing about the difficulty readers and critics encounter in dealing with minority discourses' "rhetoric of particularism" (a term synonymous with "specificity" as used throughout this study), addresses the issue of the critical application of "the death of the author" in dealing with minority texts. Sommer writes,

> If the notion of an author behind a text . . . seems naive for those of us who understand the evaporating effect of writing, we should hesitate before dismissing the ghost. Incorporeal and vulnerable precisely to our dismissive habits, authors nevertheless take positions which a responsible reading ought to respect. To locate position and difference is not to account for the difficulties of a text, or worse, to explain them away. It is to establish the kind of regard that interferes with assimilation. (Sommer, *Proceed* 26–27)

Citing Anzaldúa's descriptions of her writing process, Gagnier concludes that she "appeals to an artistic 'self' that has all the trappings of romanticism. . . . Her testimony to the difficulty and pain of genius does not differ from similar expressions throughout the annals of canonical male literature" (Gagnier 138). This assertion disregards Anzaldúa's position in relation to writing and to language itself. As a Chicana, her struggle with language, not in the sense of lacking proficiency but in the sense of being made aware of the differential power relations between her languages as well as the ways in which the hegemonic censures and delegitimizes her use of language, makes her writing process one quite different from that of white male writers. Nancy Hartstock elucidates this type of problematic application of current theoretical models in asking, "Why is it that just at the moment when so many of us who have been silenced begin to demand the right to name ourselves, to act as subjects rather than objects of history, that just then the concept of subjecthood becomes problematic?" (Hartstock 163).

Gagnier's review essay also demonstrates the danger of scholarship that in imposing inappropriate paradigms or inappropriately applying models without discussion of difference can lead to "discursive colonization." For example, Chandra Talpade Mohanty has described the tendency of some First World, white, feminist scholars to posit themselves as "knowledgeable," "liberated," "modern," and so on by seeing the Third World woman as occupying the opposite space. Yet another aspect of this "discursive colonization" is the application of an evolutionary model to feminism. Various critics have pointed out Western feminism's associations with colonialism, which Barbara Harlow summarizes as having "at times assumed for itself the prerogative of the exemplary 'civilizing mission' of its own colonial past" (Harlow quoted in Weed, xxv).[10]

Gagnier engages in this type of colonization in arguing that "although many feminists no longer emphasize their individual uniqueness, talent, or difference from others, some—especially women of color in positions of greatest vulnerability—still cling to more traditional, even romantic conceptions of the artist and the self" (Gagnier 147). This kind of rhetoric implies a feminism (white) that is located at a more advanced point in a presumed line of progression. Women of color, if we pursue this argument, occupy a less developed or less enlightened point on this line and should rely on the guidance of the more sophisticated (white) feminist.

Of course, Gagnier's essay is not itself representative of feminism, or of a feminist perspective. The very term *feminism* is misleading in its singularity, since there are at least as many feminisms as there are feminists. Rather, Gagnier's essay is taken here to demonstrate the many ways a text such as *Borderlands* can be read to force the text into compliance with preferred reading strategies and critical conventions. The intended purpose here is to analyze why these types of readings occur, that is, to identify the problems and inadequacies with the very institutions that shape and govern scholarship. If, as Gagnier's piece suggests, certain texts resist readings that employ conventional or dominant theoretical paradigms, then an investigation of how these paradigms are constructed, as well as how these constructions are influenced by exclusionary practices, could point the way toward better crosscultural communication and a better informed and more inclusive criticism.

In contrast to Gagnier's exceptionalism reading of *Borderlands,* some critics, including Chicanas/os, have pointed out what they believe to be essentialist representations in the text, particularly in regard to "the Indian Woman." Once again, a contextualization can help us to locate the text and its use of representations of the indigenous in historical, cultural, and critical perspective. Implicit in Anzaldúa's conceptualization of *mestizaje* is the figure of the Indian woman. As mentioned earlier, the term *mestizaje,* in its most literal and reductive definition, refers to miscegenation between Spanish (white, European) and Indian. In this union, the Indian woman is, whether named or unnamed, present. The necessity of this union being Spanish man/Indian woman is obvious if we consider history and the fact that when the Spanish invaded the New World, only men stepped out of their ships. Thus, any historically located discussion of *mestizaje* implies another discussion, often suppressed, on the representation of the Indian woman.

In *Borderlands,* the Indian woman is constructed as an active agent in history and in the present. Anzaldúa traces steps backward to pre-Columbian Aztec/Mexica representations of the feminine and cites evidence of the reality of the lives of women prior to and following the conquest. She simultaneously pulls forward to the position the Indian woman occupies in the culture at the present time. Anzaldúa also acknowledges the Indian woman within herself and how her "Indianness" marks her as a target for oppression within her own culture as well as that of North America at large. Racial stratification in Mexican and Chicano culture is well documented, whereby skin color and Indian features function as signifiers. To be *prieta* as opposed to *güera* signifies more than mere physical description, as both Anzaldúa and Cherríe Moraga, among others, have articulated.[11]

In U.S. culture, physical evidence of racial makeup is equally, if not more so, a marker for stratification and differential treatment. Recent sociological research reveals a significant correlation between phenotype and wages. According to Edward E. Telles, "dark and Native-American-looking Mexican origin individuals sampled in the National Chicano Survey receive substantially lower earnings than their light and European-looking counterparts" (Telles 121). Further research conducted by Dávila, Baharana, and Saenz points out that Telles's study did not take speech accent into consideration. Their study correlates speech accents and wage earnings, concluding that "independent of English proficiency, Mexican Americans speaking English with an accent tend to earn significantly lower wages than their non accented peers. . . . The employer finds an accent a more reliable indicator of an individual's origin than the person's immigration documentation" (Dávila, Baharana, and Saenz 903). These studies provide evidence of discrimination based on both racial makeup, signified by skin color, and language. Both factors are perceived to be markers of "alien" status, even superseding legal documentation.

If skin color and language function as markers, not only of difference, which is a neutral term, but of differential status, gender further stratifies and complicates the relationship of the individual within the Chicano community as well as within U.S. culture. As mentioned above, the construction of *mestizaje* as the hegemonic in parts of Latin America played a strategic unifying role in the movements of independence. Norma Alarcón likens it to the "melting pot" paradigm espoused in the United States; the key difference being the privileging of *mestizaje* in Latin America, and

Mexico in particular, versus the privileging of the white Anglo as the ideal in U.S. culture (Alarcón, "Chicana Feminism").

Yet, the idealization of *mestizaje* in nation formation in Mexico was and is based on the denial and suppression of the Indian woman. In Mexican history and culture, the native woman is constructed through the nineteenth and twentieth centuries as the monstrous double of the Virgin of Guadalupe. Guadalupe, who is represented as a mestiza, her figure emblazoned on banners carried into battles for independence, a symbol of the nation itself, is a syncretism of the goddess of fertility and sensuality, Tonatzín, and the Virgin Mary (Bartra 42–45). Through her, the native woman is appropriated and the "barbarous" within her projected onto Malintzín. Thus, "as a political compromise between conquerors and conquered, Guadalupe is the neorepresentative of the Virgin Mary and the native goddess Tonatzín, while Malintzín stands in the periphery of the new patriarchal order and its sociosymbolic contract" (Alarcón, "Traddutora" 58–59). Known as "the tongue," Malintzín was Cortes's translator as well as his concubine. Disparagingly referred to as La Malinche or La Chingada [The Fucked One], she is scripted as a traitor to her people through both her language and her body.[12]

By recognizing and naming the native woman as part of herself, Anzaldúa turns the discourse used against women to police their bodies and their language back against those who have wielded it as a weapon as well as those who have internalized it and used it against themselves and other women. Reappropriating and reterritorializing the native woman symbolized in La Malinche, Anzaldúa states,

> Not me sold out my people but they me. Because of the color of my skin they betrayed me. The dark-skinned woman has been silenced, gagged, caged, bound into servitude with marriage, bludgeoned for 300 years, sterilized and castrated in the twentieth century. For 300 years she has been a slave, a force of cheap labor, colonized by the Spaniard, the Anglo, by her own people (and in Mesoamerica her lot under the Indian patriarchs was not free of wounding). (Anzaldúa 21)

By contextualizing Anzaldúa's use of the native woman, we can see that it bears similarities with what Gayatri Spivak terms "strategic essentialism" employed in a scrupulously visible political interest (Yarbro-Bejarano 205). In a Chicana context, as Alarcón writes,

> the strategic invocation and recodification of "the" native woman in the present has the effect of conjoining the historical repression of

> the "non-civilized" dark woman—which continues to operate through "regulative psychobiographies" of good and evil women such as that of Guadalupe, Malinche, Llorona and many others—with the present moment of speech that counters such representations. (Alarcón, "Chicana Feminism" 252)[13]

Through the figure of La Malinche, the Chicana's language and body become the sites of treason. Anzaldúa subverts and negates this construct by refusing to tame her "wild tongue" in the face of "linguistic terrorism" from both sides. As a lesbian, Anzaldúa also reconfigures her body as a site of treason.[14] Chicanas have long been accused of *malinchismo,* in a heterosexist context, for sleeping with white men. As a lesbian, Anzaldúa is also aligned with La Malinche by removing her body from circulation among Chicano men.[15] Once again, Anzaldúa uses her identification with La Malinche and turns it back against that discourse through her denouncement of homophobia: "Not me sold out my people but they me."

Anzaldúa's discourse on the Indian woman is actually a form of what we can term *inversionismo. Invertir* is to turn upside down, or to turn inside out. Either one of these meanings, or both of them simultaneously, can be applied to the process by which *Borderlands* constructs a new script for the Indian woman, as well as for the "New Mestiza." The text inverts the figure of the Indian woman personified in La Malinche and reveals what is hidden below. Anzaldúa also pulls herself inside out, so to speak, in revealing the Indian woman within herself and tracing and naming her presence on her very skin.

The term *inversionismo* is also resonant in Anzaldúa's discourse on sexuality, since *invertida* is a slang term for lesbian.[16] The term *invert* to describe a homosexual, male or female, came from pseudoscientific writing in the late nineteenth century. This medical discourse, which pathologized homosexuality, was also linked to racial discourses of the time.[17] As Judith Raiskin summarizes, "categories of sexual behavior and identity created by nineteenth- and twentieth-century sexologists were also influenced by the classification systems of race, whereby people of color, particularly 'mixed race' people, and homosexuals were conflated through the ideas of evolution and degeneration prevalent in the late nineteenth century" (Raiskin 157). Anzaldúa's *inversionismo* works this discourse of racial and sexual degeneracy and turns it back on itself so that the mestiza (half-breed) and the lesbian (invert) become privileged sites. Thus, through *inversionismo,* Anzaldúa turns the discourse used against her upside down and inside out while engaging in discursive self-formation and transformation. That is *invirtiendo,* or investing in a future return or growth.

Although *Borderlands* is unmistakably grounded in a specific historical, cultural, and geographic location, as its languages make clear, particular reading strategies are still capable of wrenching it from its context and universalizing its content. Such readings necessitate the suppression of the text's discursive practices, since these cannot be universalized. Read in isolation from the other texts with which *Borderlands* is in dialogue, as well as the unwritten cultural and historical iconographies that the text subverts, it is almost inevitable that terms such as *border* and *mestiza* be read as abstractions and therefore easily grafted onto the reader's own experiential and critical framework. Elizabeth Spelman has coined this as "boomerang perception" whereby "I look at you and come back to myself" (Spelman 12).

As Yarbro-Bejarano states, regarding this type of misreading: "If every reader who identifies with the border-crossing experience described by Anzaldúa's text sees her/himself as a 'New mestiza,' what is lost in terms of the erasure of difference and specificity?" (Yarbro-Bejarano 8). Engaging in this type of appropriation neutralizes the text and carries the added benefit, or liability (depending on how we interpret it), of providing an illusion of having included a deferentially positioned perspective. It is a form of what Caren Kaplan has termed "academic tourism," and what Yarbro-Bejarano has renamed, in relation to *Borderlands,* as becoming "boarders at the border" (Yarbro-Bejarano 22).

Various critics have pointed out that discussions of "difference" without any real recognition or articulation of difference, and more importantly without the responsibility of re-evaluating or reconfiguring models based on knowledge or insight gained, is tantamount to superficial incorporation and recolonization. Anzaldúa's language requires that the reader constantly face and engage with difference. It refuses to translate and instead demands "to be met halfway" (Anzaldúa, preface). Readings that erase or neutralize difference require a form of amnesia, since the text must be reconstructed as monolingual, its discursive practices forgotten, before the reader can appropriate it as her/his own.

Readings of *Borderlands* that ignore its languages facilitate interpretations that decontextualize, essentialize, exceptionalize, and/or universalize. To perform such readings we must assume that the reader skips over those portions of the text he/she does not recognize. This practice implies a belief, on some level, that these portions are somehow irrelevant, or at least nonessential to the text as a whole. This practice is a reflection of the marginal status of Spanish and Spanglish in U.S. culture. It is on the one hand a form of academic arrogance that can justify a partial reading of a text, even when training in literary studies emphasizes close readings.

On the other hand, it can also be interpreted as a reflection of the muting of Spanish and Spanglish—and by extension the invisibility of the Spanish- or Spanglish-speaking subject—itself a form of denial employed in maintaining U.S. metaphorical and linguistic borders. In either case, readings of *Borderlands* that do not engage with its languages prevent the possibility of transformational readings that can effect changes in individual reading practices as well as institutional changes that may allow for real inclusion and diversity in scholarship and the curriculum.

Borderlands/La Frontera has reached a broad readership in the academic marketplace, albeit not as extensive as we might wish. It has been included in primarily graduate but also a few undergraduate courses within Chicano Studies and Women's Studies, and in courses in English as well as Spanish departments. The book has been taught at a full range of institutions, from the elite such as Stanford, Yale, Brown, and Cornell, to state universities such as Ohio State and the University of Arizona, as well as smaller universities and colleges throughout the United States. It is even found as part of a graduate theory course at the prestigious art school, Rhode Island School of Design. The book has been a publishing success for Aunt Lute, which is continuously selling out of each edition it prints. Yet, as encouraging as these facts may be, it is not all good news. For example, it is primarily taught in so-called special topics courses, as opposed to required courses intended to be foundational. It is also very rarely taught in undergraduate or even graduate courses that are introductory or general topic. And, more rarely still is it taught as part of a course on multiculturalism.

The preferred representative Chicano autobiographical text at the undergraduate level is, unfortunately, Richard Rodríguez's *Hunger of Memory*. It is unfortunate that Richard Rodríguez's *Hunger of Memory* is considered representative because, although the book is well written and expresses some interesting and complex points, it reflects by and large a conservative, assimilationist perspective.[18] The book, for example, takes a stand against bilingual education and affirmative action as well as relegates Spanish exclusively to the "private sphere." There are, however, opportunities for teaching Rodríguez's text in tandem with Anzaldúa's. Both engage issues of language(s), the public and the private, the fluidity of identities, and the implications, possibilities, and limits of ethnic autobiography, to name but a few points of intersection that the texts approach from radically different perspectives. Teaching, or reading, both texts together opens opportunities for them to dialogue with one another, thereby easing the tendency to make minority discourse univocal.

While getting texts such as *Borderlands* into the curriculum is itself an important goal, we must resist becoming complacent once that is achieved. We know that *how* a text is taught is as important if not more so than *what* text is taught. A course syllabus can accurately reflect the latter but is rarely an indication of the former. We can look toward scholarship on the text for critical trends and preferred readings, assuming that critical materials inform pedagogical practices. But here we run into problems of institutional power inequities that perpetuate certain critical conventions and limit publishing access to less empowered scholars.

Even fields such as Women's Studies and Cultural Studies, which are committed to revising both the canon and critical conventions, engage in exclusionary practices at the institutional level. Scholarship in Women's Studies, for example, is regulated through publication in two leading journals in the field: *Signs* and *Feminist Studies.* As Maxine Baca Zinn et al. in their article "The Cost of Exclusionary Practices in Women's Studies" have pointed out, the editorial boards of these two journals are composed almost exclusively of white women working at elite institutions, which further limits their involvement with women of color as either students or faculty. As the study concludes, "The major implication . . . is that women of color are rarely sitting around the table when problems are defined and strategies suggested" (Zinn et al. 32). The fields of Women's Studies and Feminist/Gender Theory have also been critiqued for including women of color but, due to their relatively small numbers, solely as oppositional voices.[19] Emma Pérez observes that "women of color have been invited, but not to discourse with each other. They have been invited as reactors and resisters, who reveal discursive and territorial colonization, upon entering confrontations that presume equal sociopolitical relations between first- and third-world people" (Pérez 111).

Pérez summarizes the point in stating, "Marginalized others are silenced, having no rights to spaces to construct creative rather than reactive discourses" (Pérez 111). This echoes Arias and Beverley's point regarding subalterity and representation in discussing Menchú's *testimonio.* This is not surprising given that Anzaldúa, like Menchú and Esperanza in Behar's *Translated Woman* (as well as, to some extent, Behar herself) can all be said to be "ethnicized subjects." Arias defines this term as "individuals who identify themselves with a group or community that considers itself, and is regarded by others, as culturally distinct from other, more powerful groups inhabiting the same national space" (Arias 75). "Ethnicized subjects" have been granted a place in the hegemonic, but solely as either objects of study or as respondents to dominant discourses. As critics and teachers we have been resistant to reading texts by ethnicized subjects on their own terms. To do so requires that we closely examine, revise, and at times discard conventional reading, critical, and pedagogical practices. Close engagement with texts such as Anzaldúa's, which demands to be met halfway, can lead to such revisions.

Given such a potential, what can we make of the critical avoidance of the interplay of languages in *Borderlands,* its most marked signpost of specificity? What is at stake in the ways we read this text? Arguably, what is at stake is the stability of language dominance, as well as the stability of the institutions, such as academe, which regulate the dissemination of knowledge. Engagement with the text's languages necessitates the opening of a transformational space that puts into question differential power relations in terms of race, gender, class, and sexualities through the deployment of language as a form of resistance.

Borderlands/La Frontera, in speaking from both literal and conceptual borderlands, exposes the artificiality of monolithically constructed categories. Its use of language(s) is perhaps its more obvious destabilizing strategy, but its content is equally reflective of a refusal to accept regulative forms of classification and containment. The text chooses instead to explore the space of multiple intersections. As Anzaldúa writes, "to survive the borderlands you must live *sin fronteras,* be a crossroads." Given that the coyote, too, is a border dweller, her/his identity predicated on location at the point of contact, but whose role by its very nature makes borders permeable, unstable, we can see how Anzaldúa's text can lead us to possibilities for our own research and pedagogies.

While our job as coyotes begins with transporting texts, it is also presumably our mission to transport alternative experiences, languages, histories, ways of knowing, and ways of being in the world, all of which are delegitimized, silenced, or otherwise stamped as "undocumented" by the normative drive of educational institutions. If we recognize that our roles as coyotes often make us participants in maintaining consensus and dissipating possibilities for structural change, then we can also recognize that as coyotes we can be tricksters, free to explore the possibility of exploiting our position as border dwellers, as insider/outsider.

5

Coming of Age in the Curriculum

The House on Mango Street and *Bless Me, Ultima* as Representative Texts

Since the late 1960s, there has been a growing current of debate within the humanities surrounding the canon. This current has had visible effects on the curriculum as evidenced by the institutionalization and growth of programs in areas such as Black Studies, Women's Studies, Chicano Studies, Latino Studies, and so on. Recently, there has been a trend within traditional programs, such as English, involving curriculum revisions resulting in departments not only offering more courses emphasizing works by minority writers but actually requiring students to complete a minimum of course work centering on issues of gender, race, and class. While these changes have been interpreted as too radical and accused of "political correctness" by conservative factions, others have described them as superficial, implemented for the purpose of stabilizing institutions in the face of growing dissent and militancy from disenfranchised groups.[1]

These curricular debates have tended to center around the term *multiculturalism.* There exists a great body of work arguing the term's definitions, parameters, pedagogical practices, and political implications. This ongoing debate has even moved from the usual academic settings of departmental meetings, professional journals, and books published by university presses to candidate speeches, mass media, and mainstream publishers. Take, for example, Pat Buchanan's speech during the 1992 Republican National Convention, which employed military rhetoric to rally support in fighting the "culture wars" being waged against "American" values and traditions—a war "over the hearts and minds of the American people." Specific attacks on curricular reform have also appeared in book form. These books have been marketed for a mainstream audience that is not necessarily academic. Titles such as *Cultural Literacy: What Every*

American Needs to Know (Houghton Mifflin, 1987) by E. D. Hirsch, *Tenured Radicals: How Politics Has Corrupted Higher Education* (Harper Collins, 1990) by Roger Kimball, and *The Closing of the American Mind* (Simon and Schuster, 1987) by Allan Bloom received media attention, reflecting a broader public anxiety regarding contested definitions of history, art, and culture in an American (U.S.) context.[2]

These reactions to curricular debates and revisions can be described as a backlash against a perceived erosion of a common ground in the construction, representation, and reproduction of knowledge within institutions of higher learning. In denouncing multiculturalism as politically motivated, the voices of the backlash re-edify the Eurocentric, white, male, and middle-class values. This position proposes the white, male, middle-class perspective as the apolitical, naturalized norm.[3] We take these arguments seriously, given their prominence in discourses both within and outside of academe. First, we must examine how multiculturalism is being defined. Then we must look at how and to what extent it has been implemented in curricular reform, and finally question the legitimacy of Bloom, Kimball, and Hirsch's worries, regardless of whether or not we share their political positions as defenders of the canon.

Because definitive and fully inclusive answers to these questions are well beyond the scope of a single chapter, or a single volume for that matter, this study focuses on the circulation of two texts: *Bless Me, Ultima* by Rudolfo Anaya and *The House on Mango Street* by Sandra Cisneros. Both have become "representative" of Chicano and Latina/o literature. This chapter attempts to plot the position of these texts in the multicultural matrix using as coordinates key factors in their reception. These factors are here identified as *degree of intelligibility,* which corresponds to a given text's approachability through existing paradigms and methodologies, and relative flexibility for incorporation through *manageable difference.* In other words, this chapter examines how and to what extent these two texts are incorporated as additives to the already established canonical tradition and looks at the logic behind their promotion as documented, legal trespassers into the academic landscape.

Peter McLaren identifies four forms of multiculturalism: conservative, liberal, left-liberal, and critical. The first, conservative multiculturalism, is defined by its drive to construct a common culture, using the term *diversity* "to cover up the ideology of assimilation that undergirds its position. In this view, ethnic groups are reduced to 'add-ons' to the dominant culture. Before you can be 'added on' to the dominant United States culture you must first adopt a consensual view of culture and learn to accept the essentially Euro-American patriarchal norms of the 'host' country" (McLaren 49). This particular form of multiculturalism is also linked to the process Renato Rosaldo has described as "cultural stripping." This entails that individuals shed or strip their former cultures in order to become "transparent" American citizens (Rosaldo, *Culture*).

A second form of multiculturalism, as described by McLaren, is the liberal approach or definition. This form is closely identified with "universalistic humanism in which legitimating norms which govern the substance of citizenship are identified most strongly with Anglo-American cultural-political communities" (McLaren 51). The third form, left-liberal multiculturalism, differs from both conservative and liberal forms in its emphasis on difference. However, "work within this perspective [has] a tendency to essentialize cultural differences . . . and ignore the historical and cultural 'situatedness' of difference" (McLaren 52).

Critical multiculturalism rejects the conservative and liberal forms on the grounds that they stress sameness. That is, they focus on the ways that "we are all the same after all." Critical multiculturalism, however, also takes issue with the left-liberal emphasis on difference. Both the highlighting of sameness and the highlighting of difference present the same problem. According to McLaren, both of these emphases suffer from "essentialist logic: in both, individual identities are presumed to be autonomous, self-contained and self-directed" (McLaren 53).

In place of this, critical perspectives situate representations of race, class, and gender in contexts of social struggle where meaning is constructed and deconstructed in specific histories and power relations. Critical multiculturalism does not simply emphasize "textual play or metaphoric displacement as a form of resistance, (as in the case of left-liberal multiculturalism)" but rather moves beyond it to interrogate "the construction of difference and identity in relation to a radical politics" (McLaren 53).

Locating the reception of these two representative texts on McLaren's graph points to a shifting plotting point between conservative and liberal quadrants, with an occasional bow toward a left-liberal position, but only as this third form conforms to the requisites of conservative and liberal forms. What is generally lacking from the use of these texts as representative in pedagogical and critical practices is an emphasis "positioned against the neo-imperial romance with monoglot ethnicity grounded in a shared or 'common' experience of 'America' that is associated with conservative and liberal strands of multiculturalism" (McLaren 53). That is, conservative and liberal strands of multiculturalism do not challenge the melting pot paradigm, and these tend to be the approaches used in working with these texts.

Referring to *Bless Me, Ultima* and *The House on Mango Street* as representative texts does not carry the implication that they encompass sole and complete representation of Chicano or Latino literary expression. The term *representative* is here used as reflective of existing institutional practices that overwhelmingly include one or both of these texts to the exclusion of others. These texts become representative, then, by often being the only Latina/o works assigned in a relatively broad spectrum of courses. For example, one or both are frequently the only Latina/o texts included or excerpted on Multicultural Literature and Contemporary American Literature syllabi.[4]

That these texts and their respective authors share striking similarities may be a first step in explaining their reception, yet even these similarities cannot fully account for their selection over others. For example, both Anaya and Cisneros have strong ties to universities. Anaya holds a Ph.D. and retired as professor emeritus after thirty years of service at the University of New Mexico. Cisneros is a graduate of the Iowa Creative Writing Program, where she wrote and workshopped *The House on Mango Street* as a student. While there is no doubt that both these writers' relationships with academia inform their work, this cannot account for their works' relative prominence within that context, since most Latina/o authors share similar connections. Alberto Ríos, Helena Maria Viramontes, Tomás Rivera, Ana Castillo, Judith Ortiz Cofer, Rolando Hinojosa, to name a few, are all examples of writers connected with institutions of higher learning. In fact, we would be hard pressed to name a handful who would be excluded from this list. Although some have argued that this is a situation specific to Chicanos and Latinos, it is probably more a reflection of the institutionalization of writing in general in the United States.[5]

Marketing forces yield similarly ambivalent results in terms of their explanatory potential since both works were initially published by small presses—*Bless Me, Ultima* was published with Tonatiuh and *Mango Street* was originally published with Arte Público—with limited distribution and resources. Nor can we credit the authors themselves as promoting these works as representative texts. Cisneros actively resists the label, as evidenced by her refusal to allow publication of excerpts from *Mango Street* in the *Norton Anthology of American Literature* as a protest against the editors' exclusion of other Latina and Latino voices. Anaya is similarly involved in broadening rather than narrowing literary representation. He has worked as an editor, providing publication access to less-recognized authors as well as establishing and funding "La Casita," which provides writers—particularly Chicanas and Chicanos—with room and board while completing creative projects.

Having ruled out or severely restricted the roles of institutionalization through ties with the university literary establishment, marketing and publishing forces, and self-promotion on the parts of the authors, let us return to the set of factors previously hypothesized as bearing relevance to these texts becoming established as representative. The first of these, intelligibility, is here defined as the degree to which a given text is accessible to a given community of readers based on that community's prior knowledge and expectations deployed in making meaning and assigning value. Critical work on speech act theory and reader response informs this term as well as its application in this chapter to the reception of *Bless Me, Ultima* and *The House on Mango Street.*[6]

As the discipline of linguistics has demonstrated, all units of language are necessarily incomplete or open. No utterance or written text is free of ambiguity. In the case of the written text, undecidability is further complicated in that body language or physical expressions are absent as contextual clues, and clarification on the part of the speaker is simply not an option. The negotiation of meaning, then, is removed from the speaking or writing subject and transferred to the text, so that interaction is contextualized through the reader's prior experience and knowledge of other written texts. Intelligibility, then, hinges on the extent to which a reader is able to make use of this prior knowledge or, to use Jonathan Culler's terminology, to perform "reading competence."[7]

In this regard, both of the texts under consideration can be argued to conform to a high degree of intelligibility in terms of both language and content. Most notably, they both fall into the category of the bildungsroman, or coming-of-age novel. This particular genre, deeply rooted in the conventions and formulas of a patriarchal and individualistic tradition, draws both of these texts into a specific intertextual framework. Culler's "competent reader" can then plug into this familiar framework and fill in the interstitial spaces that Anaya's and Cisneros's bicultural works make fluid and unstable. In other words, the reader possesses a thematic map of the bildungsroman, drawn to specifications embedded in a predominantly white, male system of cultural values and artistry. The reader, then, is competent to navigate these "other" texts with a diminished level of frustration. Anaya's novel is particularly well suited for grafting onto the bildungsroman cartography, while Cisneros's book (given the protagonist's gender as well as its structure as a story cycle) is more flexibly aligned with the form.

The term *bildungsroman* is applied here as it has been defined and used in English literary studies, as opposed to its somewhat different and more specific application in Germanic studies.[8] Jerome Buckley's appropriation of the term as the novel of youth or apprenticeship, a definition expanded and detailed by Randolph Shaffer, is used here as the model of the bildungsroman as it has been understood in relation to an English language tradition.

According to this model, the protagonist moves through various stages of maturity, encountering tests that lead to a fulfillment of potential and the formation of a self capable of reconciling the individual with a larger social order. *Bless Me, Ultima* follows this master plot closely, even while simultaneously articulating a Chicano mythopoetics with strong ties to indigenous New Mexico culture and cosmologies.

The novel opens with the protagonist, Antonio, first learning about Ultima, la Grande, leaving the *llano* and coming to live with his family on the outskirts of town. This marks the beginning of his apprenticeship, in the most literal sense, as Ultima's assistant. The tests that compose his progressive initiation into both Ultima's magic and the larger society include his witnessing the violence of a man shot and killed, his becoming the focal point of the struggle between the destructive magic of the *brujas* and Ultima's power, and his encounter with the Giant Carp—an important turning point in the boy's coming to spiritual understanding.

In addition to adhering to the master plot of the bildungsroman, *Bless Me, Ultima* also fulfills the set of presuppositions that Shaffer identifies as corollaries of the genre:

> 1. The idea that living is an art which the apprentice may learn.
>
> 2. The belief that a young person can become adept in the art of life and become a master.
>
> 3. The key notion of choice.
>
> 4. The prerequisite of potential for development into a master.
>
> 5. An affirmative attitude toward life as a whole. (Schaffer 18)

While the novel bears out all of these presuppositions, it does so within historical, societal, and economic parameters. In the world of the novel, the privileged reality is the one constructed by and through the immediate community. This reality does not deny the existence of a larger society, nor the differential locations of power—as in the passages relating to the racism encountered at school. Value, rather, is placed first and foremost in the context of the Chicano community—its order, values, and internal cohesion.

Within these parameters, Antonio struggles with a multiplicity of choices. For example, at his birth Antonio's maternal family, the Lunas, desire to have the child follow their traditions of farming: "And to show their hope they rubbed the dark earth of the river valley on the baby's forehead, and they surrounded the bed with the fruits of their harvest so the small room smelled of fresh green chile and corn, ripe apples and peaches, pumpkins and green beans" (Anaya 6).

In conflict with this is the paternal family, the Márez, and their wish to make him a vaquero: "And they smashed the fruits and vegetables that surrounded the bed and replaced them with a saddle, horse blankets, bottles of whiskey, a new rope, bridles, chaps, and an old guitar. And they rubbed the stain of earth from the baby's forehead because man was not to be tied to the earth but free upon it" (Anaya 6). Further complicating the child's choices is his mother's wish that he become a priest. Settling the raging argument, Ultima intercedes. "I pulled this baby into the light of life, so I will bury the afterbirth and the cord that once linked him to eternity. Only I will know his destiny" (Anaya 7).

That Antonio's future is predestined by Ultima does not, in the logic of the novel, occlude his ability to make choices. Because Ultima keeps his destiny literally buried, Antonio's coming of age and fulfillment of that destiny is still regulated by the interplay between his will and his growing spiritual consciousness. The "key concept of choice" is present in the novel, as are the other presuppositions of the bildungsroman identified by Shaffer. This ability to be grafted onto the genre's master plot allows the reader to make meaning of the spaces in the novel that display marked differences.

According to Reed Way Dasenbrock, writing in the *PMLA*, "one could say, adapting the language of Paul Grice, that there is implicit in any act of reading a maxim of intelligibility, which is that readers—like speakers and listeners—will work to make texts as intelligible as possible. Assuming that a work makes sense and has significance, the reader will try to find that sense and significance even when they are not readily apparent" (Dasenbrock 14). This commentary bears relevance to the reception of representative texts in two ways. First, it assumes that readers will work toward making meaning, but only to a point. Second, it assumes that a reader has decided at some point, perhaps prior to reading the text, that the work "makes sense and has significance." This second assumption is problematic when we are dealing with noncanonical texts. *Sense* and *significance,* in this context, are highly contested terms. Because we cannot take for granted that the reader has made this determination, we can assume that the reader will work toward making meaning in a more limited way since she/he is more uncertain about the potential payoff for the effort.

This point becomes clearer as Dasenbrock further states that "this principle can be abused, but a skillful writer will make the reader work hard only at those moments where the work is meaningful. . . . Only by doing that work, by striving to understand a different mode of expression, are we brought up against the fact of cultural difference. If everything is translated into our terms and made readily intelligible, then our cultural categories will be reinforced, not challenged" (Dasenbrock 14).

These lines, which on the surface seem to be arguing for the pedagogical and cultural "value" of multicultural texts, contain some disturbing implications. For example, there is a differentiation between the "skillful" and the "unskillful" writer based on the degree to which the text produced requires "work" on the part of the reader—work here is defined as the negotiation of meaning when confronted with difference from hegemonic norms. Dasenbrock praises the "skillful" writer who requires the reader to work hard, but in a limited way: "only at those moments where the work is meaningful." The assumption here is that we can with confidence identify these "moments," as well as discount other "moments" in the text presumed to lack meaningfulness.

What we can begin to decipher about Dasenbrock's perspective on multiculturalism is that it falls under what Goldberg calls "weak multiculturalism." Goldberg's term, which encompasses McLaren's conservative and liberal forms, is defined as consisting of "a strong set of common, universally endorsed, centrist values to which everyone—every reasonable person irrespective of the divisions of race, class, and gender—can agree. These universal principles are combined with a pluralism of ethnic insight and self-determination provided no particularistically promoted claim is inconsistent with the core values" (Goldberg 16).

Thus far, this chapter has argued that Anaya's *Bless Me, Ultima* has become a representative text based on its high degree of intelligibility in regard to form (the novel) and content (adherence to the master plot of the bildungsroman). Yet, according to Dasenbrock's taxonomy of intelligibility, this novel is "much more difficult" than other multicultural texts due to its "aggressively bilingual mode of presentation" (Gingerich 215–16 quoted in Dasenbrock 15). He argues that, "though the novel is in English, it includes a substantial amount of Spanish, for which there is very little covert or overt translation" (Dasenbrock 15).

According to Dasenbrock, this use of code switching could be a barrier to intelligibility. Yet, Dasenbrock argues, in *Bless Me, Ultima* it is used strategically to convey a bilingual reality in which not everyone understands everything all of the time. The older generation is monolingual in Spanish and the Anglo teachers are monolingual in English. Only the children who have attended school are bilingual. This is partly correct, yet the text's use of Spanish is much more limited than the "reality" Dasenbrock argues it reflects. Translations, for example, are supplied in both covert and overt fashion.

The following lines typify the text's use of both overt and covert translation: "'It would be a great honor to provide a home for la Grande,' my mother murmured. My mother called Ultima la Grande out of respect. It meant the woman was old and wise" (Anaya 4). Note that Antonio's mother's dialogue is in English, although it is understood that she is speaking in Spanish. More subtly, the translation of "la Grande" is in fact provided. What the novel does do, which can be interpreted as "aggressive use of bilingualism," is not italicize Spanish words. By not signaling the appearance of these words, the text catches the reader off guard and causes moments of disruption in the reading process. Even so, the tension brought on by the surprise appearance of a "foreign" word is quickly dissipated as the reader regains confidence through direct or contextualized translation.

Even Dasenbrock's brief summary of the novel signals his dominant culture-centric approach. The brevity of the description, "a novel about a young Hispanic growing up in bilingual New Mexico in the 1940s" (Dasenbrock 15), is understandable, particularly since the article also discusses three other texts, yet even in its brevity it exemplifies a number of problems in multicultural critical practices. The most obvious of these is the use of the term *Hispanic,* which has a controversial history as a term brought into circulation by the U.S. Census Bureau to homogenize differences among groups such as Puerto Ricans, Chicanos, and Cuban Americans. The term is also offensive to many Chicanos because of its emphasis on Peninsular culture.[9] This lumping together of various distinct groups with specific cultures, histories, and modes of expression also blurs important racial and class-based distinctions within groups.[10] Such generalization is particularly dangerous in the case of a writer such as Anaya who writes from a specific location as a New Mexico Chicano mestizo, with special emphasis on his indigenous heritage.

Secondly, Dasenbrock's "young Hispanic" lacks gender, and although the protagonist's gender is unmarked (not female), it certainly is significant, as will become obvious when we compare *Bless Me, Ultima* to *Mango Street*. These crucial oversights become even more disturbing in light of the fact that the article appeared in the *PMLA*, which is indicative of the lack of participation of multiculturalists with a more critical bent on editorial boards at elite publications. Not surprisingly, this was the first article on Latina/o literature published in the *PMLA*.[11] Furthermore, it is not dedicated solely to a Latina/o text, but to the broad label of multiculturalism.

Herein lies the danger of blanket terms such as *multiculturalism*. Through normative institutional practices, the term allows for a recognition of "difference," yet because the term itself is overdetermined, it provides opportunities for exploitative uses of marginalized texts. These uses can function as strategies of containment, which on the one hand acknowledge the cultural specificity of texts such as *Bless Me, Ultima* and *Mango Street* but regulate their oppositional or transformational potentialities by requiring "manageable differences" as conditional to acceptance.

In these two texts, the fact that they are both narrated through the voices of children is exemplary of manageable difference, whereby misinformation and stereotypes can be re-edified. These two texts in and of themselves do not engage in stereotypic representations, yet because they have become representative, their portrayals of characters and community life are easily generalized. The child narrator in particular facilitates problematic readings of Chicanas and Chicanos as childlike, which undercuts anxiety regarding the policing of minority individuals and communities. In other words, these two texts, read outside of a fuller context of inclusion that would provide opportunities for recognition of diversity within diversity, foster an illusion of communities that are not only nonthreatening to the dominant society, but also by association with the child narrator, less knowing, less experienced, and less empowered than the adult reader.

Sandra Cisneros's *Mango Street* can, like Anaya's novel, be classified as a bildungsroman, but due to gender, and to some extent form, it imposes itself on the cartography of the genre more resistantly, pushing and stretching boundaries in all directions. The gender difference in the bildungsroman, most critics agree, turns on the concept of choice, and "even the broadest definitions of the bildungsroman presuppose a range of social options available only to men" (Abel et al. 7).

While the male protagonist of the genre undergoes a process of education to become a "master," for the female protagonist an education as to her function and role in society leads her in the opposite direction, toward subservience. And, as Anais Pratt points out, whereas in rites of passage, adolescent males undergo tests in valor and strength, younger girls are given "tests in submission" (Pratt, A. 14). Thus gender problematization is built in to the *Bildung* the moment it is undertaken by a female protagonist. That in Cisneros's book this protagonist is a working-class Chicana further interrogates the presuppositions of the genre's universal tenets.

Yet, even as a revision of the genre, *Mango Street* offers a veneer of familiarity in its association with coming-of-age books. As in other works of the genre, the protagonist of Cisneros's book, Esperanza, undergoes a process of individuation, constructing a self in relation to and in opposition from others. In connection to this process of individuation, and a requisite of the bildungsroman, is the protagonist's physical removal from family and community in the form of a departure. In the conventional bildungsroman, the completion of a formal education prompts the protagonist's leaving home. There is a promise of this in the final vignette of *The House on Mango Street:* "one day I will say goodbye to Mango. I am too strong for her to keep me here forever" (Cisneros 101). But for Esperanza, leaving Mango Street in the process of individuation is neither the beginning of her apprenticeship nor the goal. Rather, the departure is seen as a step toward the return, toward reconnection or attachment: "They will not know I have gone away to come back for the ones I left behind. For the ones who cannot out" (Cisneros 102).

This going away to return, or seeking distance as a step toward reunion and public responsibility, is reflective of an alternative Chicano tradition of the bildungsroman exemplified by writers such as Tomás Rivera in his classic work *. . . y no se lo tragó la tierra* [*And the Earth Did Not Devour Him*]. This alternative tradition, informed by the ideology of the Chicano Movement and the emergence of a new group identity, worked toward a "decentering of individualism" (Calderón 112) through both content and experimentation in form. This experimentation has led to the widespread use of the short story cycle, a form characterized by Renato Rosaldo as "the novel's 'poor relation'" (Rosaldo, "Fables" 88) and by Héctor Calderón as "prenovelistic" (Calderón 100).[12]

Mango Street's structure as a short story cycle enables the text to "poach" elements from the bildungsroman (Gutiérrez-Jones 310) while participating in a counterhegemonic discursive tradition that works to subvert the ideology of individualism. As a critique of the novel and the social, economic, patriarchal structures that gave rise to the novel and that the genre in turn reproduces, the short story cycle relies on oral narrative traditions, matriarchal heritage, and community-centered values. Unfortunately, because this is a relatively obscure form, story cycles are often read *as if* they were novels. This leads to a disregard for the construction of meaning through form.

In the case of *Mango Street,* this disregard has led to some conflicted readings of the text. Feminist critics, for example, familiar with arguments of relationships between gender and genre have questioned the possibilities of the female bildungsroman. Feminist readings of the text have been carried out which argue the text's relation to more traditional forms of the genre. Yet, as important as establishing this text in a feminist context may be, it is also imperative to locate it within a Chicano critique of the genre through the story cycle.

As feminist critics have noted, "isolate individualism is an illusion. It is also the privilege of power. A white man has the luxury of forgetting his skin color and sex. He can think of himself as an 'individual.' Women and minorities, reminded at every turn in the great cultural hall of mirrors of their sex or color, have no such luxury" (Friedman 39). Esther Labovitz has argued that because the sanctioned social role of women has in the past precluded the search for or the existence of an individual self, there was no possibility of a female counterpart to *Bildung* prior to societal changes in the twentieth century. She goes on to argue that the evolution of the genre parallels the male *Bildung* as "cultural and social structures appeared to support women's struggle for independence" (Labovitz 70).

While this may hold true, at least to some degree, for white, middle-class women, it is questionable to assume it could be applied to women of color or, more generally, women marginalized on the basis of race, ethnicity, sexual orientation, or class (Gutiérrez-Jones 299). What Labovitz's evolutionary model is lacking is an interrogation of the construction of the autonomous individual and the desirability of the adoption of such a construct by marginalized women.

Regenia Gagnier, in a review essay of women's autobiographies in the 1980s, looks at several texts including Gloria Anzaldúa's *Borderlands/La Frontera* and Cisneros's *Mango Street* in relation to the ideology of individualism and the exceptionalization of the artist. While Gagnier does engage in a critique of the political implications such an ideology carries when adopted by women of color, she reads Cisneros and Anzaldúa as reproducing that ideology in their respective texts (Gagnier 140). As it is argued in chapter 4, such a reading is fostered through a displacement of these texts from their respective contexts and intertextual play with other discourses and traditions.[13] Gagnier, for example, does not acknowledge the structural subtext of *Mango Street* and in fact misidentifies it as an autobiography.

Mango Street negates the ideology of individualism in several ways, the most notable being that even as the narrator remains constant, the text is composed of forty-six vignettes describing and expressing the interiority of a wide spectrum of characters who make up the Mango Street neighborhood. For example, there is Mamacita for whom "home is a house in a photograph" (Cisneros 77). There is Geraldo No Last Name, whose life Esperanza, in spite of never meeting him and learning of him from someone else, can nevertheless imagine and explain: "They never saw the kitchenettes. They never knew about the two room flats and sleeping rooms he rented, the weekly money orders sent home, the currency exchanges. How could they?" (Cisneros 66). And there is Marin who dances under the streetlight, "waiting for a car to stop, a star to fall, someone to change her life" (Cisneros 27).

In the traditional bildungsroman, attention remains focused exclusively on the protagonist, while *Mango Street* disperses the spotlight to include the community as inseparable from the protagonist's identity. As the three sisters tell Esperanza: "You will always be Esperanza. You will always be Mango Street" (Cisneros 105).

Unlike the protagonist of the traditional bildungsroman, Esperanza does not travel during the course of the book, nor does the text end with an escape. This is significant in that her psychic movement from childhood to adolescence to adulthood takes place within the geographic and cultural boundaries of her community. Her individuation is undertaken, like Antonio's in *Bless Me, Ultima,* in a community-centered context, a marked difference from the master plot of the genre in which the protagonist physically travels outward. This community centeredness demonstrates a point of negotiation of the conflict, for the Latina/o author working within the bildungsroman tradition, between the valorization of the individual inherent in the genre and its incompatibility with the political and cultural implications that valorization carries for minority intellectuals.

Generalized readings of these two texts that connect them solely to the familiar mapping of the novel, and more specifically to the bildungsroman with its assumption and valorization of the autonomous individual, reduce reader frustration at moments of difference, be it content based as in Anaya's text, or structural difference as in Cisneros's. This diminished frustration leads to a higher degree of intelligibility, and the assigning of a higher status for these two texts, relative to that of other Latina/o texts. By isolating these texts from their discursive and historical contexts, they can also function as mirrors of the hegemonic and confirmations of stereotypic representations. Thus, it is not the texts themselves that are problematic, since they do engage in layered critiques and propose their own aesthetics. Rather, it is their acceptance as representative that is troubling, given that they do provide opportunities for easy incorporation, which erases their transformative possibilities.

Conclusion

Coyotes in the Classroom

Institutions of higher learning are continuously adapting to the changing needs of "education." Because of the dynamic nature of academia, curriculum revision is not, and never will be, completed. As scholars and teachers, we are challenged to become specialists in a given field but also to wander outside of our areas of specialization—to become border crossers. This, of course, like any border crossing, carries dangers. Yet it also carries many rewards. Unlike undocumented workers who cross borders out of necessity and at great physical risk, we as academics are intentional border crossers. We choose to step outside of our prescribed areas. What we make of our border crossings is also a choice.

What this book proposes is that we not only recognize but embrace the figure of the coyote as a way to make sense of our roles as scholars and teachers. The negative connotations surrounding the figure of the coyote function to constantly remind us of our positions and lead us to accept a certain degree of responsibility in how and to what ends we transport texts across borders or boundaries.

Yet, identifying with the coyote by focusing exclusively on these negative connotations would prove to be counterproductive and even paralyzing. We would find ourselves trapped in a "Damned if you do, damned if you don't" situation. To move away from this impasse, while still embracing the identification with the coyote, necessitates an exploration of the positive and transformational possibilities.

While we put great emphasis on and feel personally vested in our research and scholarship, for most of us, the classroom is where we have the strongest impact. It is in this space that we can assume coyote identities that are liberating rather than restrictive. The coyote serves as a guide in a dangerous and high-stakes journey. This is a role quite different from that of tour guide. Thus, being the coyote in the classroom is not to be equated with facilitating "academic tourism." It is, rather, a role closely identified with critical pedagogy such as that espoused by Paulo Freire. What this conclusion proposes to do is present some suggestions for the coyote in the classroom. These are by no means exhaustive. The possibilities for transporting border crossing and border dwelling texts into academia are limited only by the creativity of individual teachers—which is to say, endless.

One of the many ways we can function as coyotes is to disrupt the relationship between center and periphery. To do this, we must go beyond simply tacking on a text from the margin to an otherwise traditional syllabus. We all know that the last text taught is often read hastily, and by this time, the more serious students are already working on papers and preparing for exams. In other words, when placed last on a syllabus, the text too often becomes an afterthought or mere footnote to the course.

A revision as simple as placing a border crossing or border dwelling text first on a syllabus addresses this problem but also works on a deeper level. Whether intentional on the part of the teacher or not, students have come to expect that the first text in a course provides the framework or structure for the entire semester (or quarter). All texts that follow, then, are read through that first or "foundational" text. Border crossing and border dwelling texts demand revisions to established reading strategies. Once students have grappled with these texts and then move on to more familiar ground, they are better able to recognize it as such.

A concrete example of this is found in an essay by Janet Verner Gunn that narrates the experience of reading and teaching *I, Rigoberta Menchú* alongside Annie Dillard's *An American Childhood*. Verner Gunn explains that reading Menchú's *testimonio* helped her and her students look deeper into what Dillard's memoir takes for granted—namely the assumptions a Western literary tradition has established regarding not only autobiography, but the very notion of selfhood. Verner Gunn's essay concludes that reading a text such as *I, Rigoberta Menchú* alongside a more familiar (in terms of both form and content) autobiographical text "calls on first-world readers to take responsibility, not for the third world but for the locatedness and therefore the limitations of our own perspective" (Gunn 278). Reading border crossing or border dwelling texts relationally, then, enriches our understanding of both the border text and the more centrally located text.

Verner Gunn's essay is part of the collection *Teaching and Testimonio* edited by Allen Carey-Webb and Stephen Benz. Other essays in this highly useful volume include descriptions of courses that teach *I, Rigoberta Menchú* in relation to a variety of texts. This demonstrates that border crossing and border dwelling texts offer great pedagogical versatility since they tend to share points of intersection with a broad spectrum of texts. For example, one of the essays in the collection points to ways to read and teach *I, Rigoberta Menchú* in relation to slave narratives.[1] Both the slave narrative and *testimonio* provide a first-person account of the reality of a member of a silenced or oppressed group. They also share an urgency in calling for political action to address an injustice.[2]

I, Rigoberta Menchú and other *testimonios* can also be used to question the very notion of "truth" and how it is represented. Carey-Webb suggests reading the text alongside U.S. media reports on the civil war in Guatemala. Benz includes other testimonial material such as Amnesty International reports and Robert Cormack's *Harvest of Violence,* which gathers testimonies and analysis by U.S. anthropologists.[3] I would also suggest including Stoll's book as a way of "teaching the conflict" regarding Menchú's book, and also as a means for students to work through for themselves conflicting perspectives and versions of "the truth."

I, Rigoberta Menchú can also be used to help students examine their own lives and guide them in constructing their own life narratives. José David Saldívar has described a popular and successful course at Stanford that uses two border texts, Anzaldúa's *Borderlands/La Frontera* and Cherríe Moraga's *Loving in the War Years,* as guides for students writing their own autobiographical narratives (Saldívar, *Border* 75).[4] *I, Rigoberta Menchú* can also be useful in this way.

Like *I, Rigoberta Menchú, Borderlands* also shares various points of intersection with differently positioned texts. Courses on Chicana/o and Latina/o literature, as well as those on women's autobiography, offer obvious opportunities for inclusion of this text. Yet, there can be many others. At Florida State University, for example, it was included in a course titled "Hispanic Margins" that covered points of cultural and linguistic contact from Medieval Peninsular literature to present day linguistic and cultural borders.

An important area where texts such as *Borderlands* should be included is Critical Theory. When we organize and present this material, we often neglect to question what counts as Theory and who has the authority to define it. Border crossing and border dwelling texts provide a means to question our assumptions and exclusionary practices in formulating our own, and our students', conceptualization of the theoretical.

Border crossing and border dwelling texts reside at intersections. This is also true of their contexts, which are always plural. That is, the texts exist in many contexts. To include all possible contexts when we read and teach these texts is, of course, impossible. As coyotes, we choose the point or points of entry. The contexts we choose to provide, however, must locate the texts in relation not only to other texts, but to their histories. It is not enough to link individual texts through generalized terms such as *marginalization* or *oppression*. We must also differentiate and define each margin and each form of oppression; or, even better, provide material for our students to think critically about these terms and what they mean in specific contexts.

This approach can alleviate problems such as the "Boom(ing) effect" discussed in chapter 2. By helping our students create contexts for "magical realism" as practiced in some Latin American works of fiction, and differentiating this from moments of "magic" in Latina/o texts in the United States, we can work toward recognizing the overlaps but also acknowledging the differences.

And finally, to move past the use of texts as representative, we must simply include more border crossing and border dwelling texts. By reading a multiplicity of diverse voices and perspectives, students are better able to resist taking a single text, or a single voice, as metonymically standing in for a heterogenous, internally diverse group.

If, for example, Richard Rodríguez's *Hunger of Memory* is included on the reading list, Anzaldúa's *Borderlands* can also be read to provide balance. The goal of providing balance is crucial in avoiding the danger of reproducing, rather than breaking down, stereotypes. As coyotes, we are responsible for providing our students the necessary tools to recognize diversity within diversity. If, for example, we teach Julia Alvarez's *How the Garcia Girls Lost their Accent*, which deals with an upper-class, white immigrant family from the Dominican Republic, we should also include authors such as Junot Díaz. His short story collection *Drown* includes issues of poverty and race in a Dominican American context. The two books, it must be noted, also address gender but come from radically different perspectives.

These are only a few suggestions for working the coyote identity into a critical and involved pedagogy. There is no magic formula, and each of us must create our own definition of the coyote in the classroom and revise that definition each time we face a new group of students. As coyotes, we must be flexible and change our routes and strategies as needs arise. But above all, we must remain passionate and hold on to our knowledge that what we do, and how we do it, are matters of great importance and consequential to our disciplines, ourselves, and our students.

Notes

Introduction

1. This is true in more ways than one. The United States exports images of itself through the entertainment industry, transnational corporations, military intervention, and foreign aid.

2. As Beverley and others have pointed out, "Latin America is to some extent now 'inside' its North American other . . . with a Hispanic population of close to thirty million, the United States is today the fifth largest country of the Spanish-speaking world" (Beverley, *Subalternity* 3).

3. Edward Said's classic text *Orientalism,* Christopher Miller's *Blank Darkness,* and Marianna Torgovnick's *Gone Primitive,* to name but a few, present sound arguments against appeals to "authenticity."

4. Nancy Fraser, quoted in Carol Boyce Davies, asserts that there are central, hegemonic discursive areas—the academy, parliament, media—and that these public spaces set boundaries on public discourse.

5. The term is borrowed from Lynne Uttal's article, "Inclusion Without Influence: The Continued Tokenism of Women of Color."

6. Donna Haraway has also explored the potential of the coyote figure to inform feminist theory (Haraway 199).

Chapter 1. Border Crossers and Coyotes

1. The term *shadow biography* was coined by the anthropologist Gayla Frank.

2. For a solid and informative summary of Border Studies in Mexico see "The Changing Face of Border Culture Studies" by Victor Zúñiga.

3. Examples of these critics' work relating to Border Theory are: "Criticism in the Contact Zone," by Mary Louise Pratt; "Worldliness-without-World, Homelessness-as-Home: Toward a Definition of the Specular Border Intellectual" (1992) by Abdul R. JanMohamed; and "The World and the Home" (1992) by Homi K. Bhabha.

4. For a full discussion and explanation of the differences between oral and written communication see Walter Ong's *Orality and Literacy: The Technologizing of the Word,* 1982.

5. The term *subaltern* refers to the economically disempowered, a person or group existing on the margins of society. It was originally a British colonial military term, used in India, to refer to the soldiers from the poorest classes who were designated as subordinate. The term was subsequently appropriated by intellectuals writing about India's postcolonial condition. The term *subaltern* has been expanded and is now widely used in other contexts, including Latin America.

Spivak argues that the subaltern are spoken about, and even spoken for, but silenced in terms of their own ability to speak a discourse that can enter hegemonic discursive areas. See her article "Can the Subaltern Speak?"

6. As an interesting side note related to the presence of multiple genres in Behar's book, *Translated Woman* has been adapted for the stage by the theater company Pregones.

7. *Fotonovelas* are story books that follow a format similar to that of a comic book. Their audience is primarily women. The plot lines are often romance stories with an element of tragedy as well as an implied moral lesson.

8. For a well-researched and compelling study of women brought before the Inquisition in colonial Mexico, see Jean Franco's *Plotting Women.* Behar cites Franco's work and was originally drawn to the town of Mexquitic to research women's Inquisition narratives.

9. A *milpa* is a small plot of land for cultivating corn.

10. Paz's use of the term *fiesta* parallels Bakhtin's use of *the carnavalesque*. Either one of these terms applies to the transgressive nature of the ceremony at the spiritist center.

11. The *comadre* relationship is founded on the request made of a woman by another to become the godmother of her child. It is important to note that a child has, aside from his/her baptismal godmother, also a communion godmother, confirmation godmother, and godmothers who contribute to special events and celebrations, such as the *madrina del pastel* or cake godmother responsible for providing the cake for a girl's *quince* or fifteenth birthday party. Thus, a woman can and usually has many *comadres.* Often, the *comadre* selected is from a different socioeconomic class, primarily one more affluent than that of the child's mother. This insures a form of sponsorship for both the child and the mother, who can expect certain gifts of favors which are part of a godmother's and a *comadre*'s responsibilities. The mother of the child, that is, the less affluent *comadre,* is in turn expected to provide small gifts such as food or handmade items as tokens for her *comadre. Comadres,* particularly if they are from disparate classes, retain formalities like using the formal terms of address such as *usted,* although they are bound to one another in responsibilities and loyalties.

12. For fuller discussions of the relationship between the West and the "Primitive," in relation to the West's construction of itself against these "Others," see Edward Said's *Orientalism,* Christopher Miller's *Blank Darkness,* and Marianna Torgovnick's *Gone Primitive.*

13. For a discussion of the link between the construction of the Malinche figure

as the Mexican Eve and ultimate traitor and the construction of Chicano nationalism through the appropriation of machismo, see Angie Chabram-Dernersesian's article, "I Throw Punches for My Race, but I Don't Want to Be a Man."

14. Norma Alarcon's article, "Traddutora, Traditora" offers an in-depth explanation of the relationship between translation and betrayal in the context of Chicana criticism.

15. Rosaldo's chapter, "Border Crossings," in *Culture and Truth,* makes a strong case against the privileging of the detached observer and argues that the practice has in fact had a negative effect on research in the social sciences by limiting it.

16. The polemics surrounding Behar's "Biography in the Shadow" are also summarized and addressed by Gayla Frank in her essay "Ruth Behar's Biography in the Shadow: A Review of Reviews."

17. The term *literary wetback* which Behar uses was originally coined by Alicia Gaspar de Alba.

Chapter 2. Boom(ing) Fictions: Magical Realism and the Reception of Latina/o Literatures

1. For outlines and discussions of the characteristics of Boom texts see Donald L. Shaw's *Nueva narrativa hispanoamericana* and J. Ann Duncan's *Voices, Visions and a New Reality.*

2. Boom novels have been criticized as not only elitist but serving the needs of metropolitan centers. See, for example, Juan Manuel Marcos's *De García Márquez al Post-Boom* and Santiago Colás's *Postmodernity in Latin America: The Argentine Paradigm.*

3. There were other voices and narrative styles concurrent with the Boom. See David William Foster's *Alternate Voices in the Contemporary Latin American Narrative.*

4. The terms *First World* and *Third World* are used in spite of their problematic connotations. The terms imply, for example, boundaries and differences that are not always rigid and intimate an internal homogeneity within each category that is illusory.

5. This was particularly true in Spain. For a discussion on the place of the Boom in Spain see Santana's *Foreigners in the Homeland.*

6. For a similar view on the superficial interpretation and application of magical realism see Neil Larson's Foreword to Emily Hicks's *Border Writing.*

7. The Ariel-Caliban debate to which Spivak alludes is based on the characters in Shakespeare's play *The Tempest.* José Enrique Rodó in the late nineteenth century proposed the figure of Ariel as the model. Roberto Fernández Retamar in his 1971 essay revises Rodó and proposes Caliban as the model, following Caribbean writers Aimé Césaire, George Lamming, and Edward Brathwaite, who take up Caliban as the symbol of the colonized Caribbean in the 1960s. The appropriation of Caliban as a symbol is explained by Retamar in his description of the character as "the deformed Caliban—enslaved, robbed of his island, and trained to speak by Prospero—rebukes

Prospero thus: 'you taught me language, and my profit on't/ Is, I know how to curse. The red plague rid you/ For learning me your language!'" (Retamar 5–6). Retamar summarizes his argument with the statement, "what is our history, what is our culture, if not the history and culture of Caliban" (Retamar 14).

8. Bell summarizes the polemics surrounding Latin America and its relation to the "postcolonial" arguing that the region's position is "eccentric" due to its being "not sufficiently white/European/imperial to be homogenized, nor sufficiently black/non-Western/colonial to be tokenized. . . . Its formal independence came too long ago, and so it has not been recently 'liberated.'" He further argues that the first two points make the region "quintessentially postcolonial," while the latter point makes it "precocious rather than belated" (Bell 25).

9. The term *American* or *America*, unless otherwise stated, is used to refer to all of the Americas.

10. Carpentier's essay first appeared as the preface to *El reino de este mundo* [*The Kingdom of this World*] and was later expanded and published in the collection of essays *Tientos y diferencias*, published in 1967. The quotes included here are from Tanya Huntington and Lois Parkinson Zamora's translation published in *Magical Realism: Theory, History, Community*.

11. See R. L. Williams's preface to *The Boom in Retrospect* for a clarification and distinction between the "new novel" which began in the 1940s and the Boom which takes place in the 1960s.

12. It must be noted that not all critics saw the Boom as a reaction or total rupture from *costumbrismo* or *criollismo*. Angel Rama in "El Boom en perspectiva" saw it as a continuation of the search for a Latin American identity began by pre-Boom authors. For a similar position, see also Inca Rumold's "Independencia cultural de Latinoamérica."

13. For evidence of the large volume of work produced on the topic of magical realism see Antonio Planellas's "La polémica sobre el realismo mágico en Hispanoamérica," which includes a comprehensive bibliography with over 125 entries. See also the "Selected Bibliography" by Zamora and Faris, the editors of *Magical Realism: Theory, History, Community*.

14. Since the publication and critical reception of Boom fiction, some critics have identified elements of magical realism in the works of non–Latin American writers such as Günter Grass, Leslie Marmon Silko, Salman Rushdie, and Toni Morrison, to name but a few. See, for example, "Magical Realism in *Midnight's Children*," by Jean-Pierre Durix; "Les romans de Jean-Louis Baghio'o et le réalisme merveilleux redéfini," by Charles Scheel; and "Naming, Magic and Documentary: The Subversion of the Narrative in *Song of Solomon, Ceremony,* and *China Men*," by Paula Rabinowitz.

15. There has been a strong reaction, particularly within Latin America, to a perceived absence of sociopolitical content in Boom novels. Boom authors themselves, as well as some critics, have argued that experimentation in form is a revolutionary act that can propel political change, yet many disagree. For early critiques of

the Boom's lack of direct engagement with politics and social change, see Hernán Vidal's "Literatura hispanoamericana e ideología liberal: surgimento y crisis," as well as the now classic and polemical work *Literatura en la revolución y revolución en la literatura* by Oscar Collazo.

16. Changes in the Hispanic publishing industry also contributed to the Boom becoming an international phenomenon. In the 1960s, Barcelona became the center of Hispanic book production, with publishers such as Seix Barral increasing the availability of books across international boundaries. For discussions of the role of the publishing industry on the Boom, see Santana's *Foreigners in the Homeland* (33–35), Angel Rama's "El Boom en perspectiva," and Alejandro Herrero-Olaizola's "Consuming Aesthetics: Seix Barral and José Donoso in the Field of Latin American Literary Production."

17. Watson is not alone in proposing this. Writing from a very different perspective, and to different ends, critics and writers have called for an end to excessive experimentation. Chilean writer Antonio Skármeta, in his essay "La novísima generación; varias características y un límite," articulates a reaction by some writers to the proliferation of experimentation fueled by the success of Boom novels. Critic Peter Earl has similarly called the drive to place craft and experimentation above all else "the cult of creative nothingness" (Earle 25).

18. While there are many different approaches to translation, most can be divided into two groups. The first of these is exemplified by Walter Benjamin's approach, which argues that a translation must always sound "foreign," reminding the reader that it is in fact a translation. The second group is exemplified by practitioners such as Pasternak, whose Russian translation of Shakespeare is generally viewed as a re-authoring of the plays as if they had been originally written in Russian for a Russian audience.

19. Emir Rodríguez Monegal identifies three phases of the Boom, the third being the "translation phase." While this third phase was based in metropolitan centers and focused on a readership outside of Latin America, Monegal argues very convincingly that the Boom was also, in its earlier phases, a product of cultural changes within Latin America, including the expansion during the postwar period of a Latin American reading public as well as the emergence of a Latin American publishing industry. For a detailed history of the Boom, as viewed within Latin America, see Monegal's book, *El Boom de la novela latinoamericana.*

20. *Ficciones* was first published in English translation, by Grove Press, in 1962. Yet, a collection of Borges's stories, including "The Garden of Forking Paths," was rejected for publication by Knopf in 1957, and *El Aleph* was likewise rejected by that publishing house in 1949. According to Knopf's records, the manuscripts were recognized as remarkable but rejected based on the assumption that they were unmarketable. See Speer Morgan et al., "Publication Is Not Recommended: From the Knopf Files."

21. For a very good discussion of translation in García Márquez's novel, see Aníbal González's "Translation and Genealogy: *One Hundred Years of Solitude.*"

22. Margaret Sayers Peden's article, "Translating the Boom: The Apple Theory of Translation," offers an interesting, linguistic-based analysis of translations of Boom novels.

23. Although Latina/o fiction writers have chosen to work almost exclusively in English, many poets such as Francisco Alarcón, Tino Villanueva, and Gustavo Pérez Firmat continue to write and publish their work in Spanish or bilingual editions.

24. More recently, publishing houses have been experimenting with Spanish translations of Latina/o texts originally written in English. Mary Helen Ponce's *Hoyt Street,* Sandra Cisneros's *The House on Mango Street,* Cristina García's *Dreaming in Cuban,* Esmeralda Santiago's *When I Was Puerto Rican,* Julia Alvarez's *How the Garcia Girls Lost Their Accent,* and Oscar Hijuelos's *The Mambo Kings Play Songs of Love* serve as examples of this.

25. Spanglish is, as the name suggests, a mixing of English and Spanish. Sometimes the mixing is done through code-switching or using both languages within one sentence. Other times grammar or word ending from one language is used in the other, as in using *yarda* for yard by adding the feminine Spanish ending to an English word.

26. The term *over-translation* as applied to bilingual Latina and Latino texts and cultural expressions is borrowed from Gustavo Pérez-Firmat.

27. Sandra Cisneros's vignette "Salvador Late or Early" appears in the anthology *Iguana Dreams: New Latino Fiction.*

28. Doris Sommer provides an analysis of bilingual humor and its effects on monolingual and bilingual readers and listeners in chapter 4 of *Proceed with Caution,* "Cortez in the Courts." Her article "Be-longing and Bi-lingual States" similarly discusses the dynamics of bilingual humor and ties the observations to bilingual reading practices.

29. Critics have pointed out Cuban Americans as the exception to this. Although the initial wave of migration from Cuba to the United States following the Revolution in 1959 was primarily white and middle- to upper-class, previous and subsequent migrations have including large numbers of working-class individuals resulting in class diversity within exile communities.

30. In contrast to the marked absence of women writers in the Boom, the years following the phenomenon, at times referred to as the post-Boom, have seen the predominance of women such as Carmen Boullosa (Mexico), Diamela Eltit (Chile), Luisa Valenzuela (Argentina), Cristina Peri Rossi (Uruguay), and Rosario Ferré and Ana Lydia Vega (Puerto Rico), to name but a few.

31. For a fuller discussion on the role of *machismo* in the Boom, see Rosario Ferré's satirical "El coloquio de las perras."

32. Ana Castillo, Sandra Cisneros, Judith Ortiz Cofer, Julia Alvarez, Cristina García, Helena María Viramontes, and Esmeralda Santiago are all to varying degrees examples of Latina writers gaining a place of relative prominence.

33. Angie Chabram-Dernersesian's "I Throw Punches for My Race, But I Don't

Want to Be a Man" provides a historicized discussion of the construction of Chicano identity through machismo.

34. While the presence or preoccupation with *crónicas* of discovery and colonization has been noted in several Boom and magical realist texts, yet another connection between the *crónicas* and the Boom is their appeal to "and dependency on 'foreign' audiences in metropolitan centers" (Bell 9).

35. Notable exceptions to the trend are found in institutions with Latino Studies and Chicano Studies programs that are well established. The institutions offer more courses and at regular intervals, providing students opportunities to study these literatures in depth.

36. The relatively easy incorporation of Latin American texts, particularly those of the Boom, across disciplines has been of utmost concern to Latin Americanists. See, for example, Bell's "Prolegomenon," Jean Franco's "Beyond Ethnocentrism: Gender, Power, and the Third-World Intelligentsia," and Doris Sommer's *Proceed with Caution.* Regarding First World critical appropriations, see also Carlos Rincón's "Modernidad periférica y el desafío de lo postmoderno: perspectivas del arte narrativo latinoamericano" and Walter Mignolo's "Canons A(nd) Cross-Cultural Boundaries (or, Whose Canon Are We Talking About?)"

Chapter 3. Out of Bounds: *Testimonio* and Its Reception

1. Stoll's book specifically questions several key points in *I, Rigoberta Menchú,* including, for example, her description of a younger brother's death from malnutrition, her witnessing another brother's death at the hands of the military, her mother's rape and death also at the hands of the military, and her father's political involvement, to name but a few.

2. The *Washington Post,* the *New York Times, Newsweek Magazine,* and other mainstream media outlets carried the story of Stoll's book as well as Menchú's statements regarding the matter.

3. It must be noted that Stoll is not the only researcher to contest Menchú's *testimonio* as transparent truth. Other anthropologists and academics have pointed out that Menchú's description of Maya Quiché culture glosses over negative aspects of the culture. For a fuller discussion of this see George Yúdice's article "*Testimonio* and Postmodernism" and Marc Zimmerman's article "*Testimonio* in Guatemala: Payeras, Rigoberta and Beyond."

4. The book also went through further editing by other members of Menchú's organization before publication, including Mario Payeras, the author of the guerrilla testimonio *Días de la selva* (1980). As Beverley writes, "in a sense, *I, Rigoberta Menchú* is thus a text produced not only by a committee but by a central committee, with specific political goals in mind" (Beverley, "The Real Thing" 286).

5. Mary Louise Pratt, in a paper delivered at the MLA convention in 1995, points out that, given that the text has undergone several printings and editions since its original publication and neither Menchú nor Burgos Debray have attempted to

change or alter this problematic introduction, we may interpret that both women have a stake in what these pages reveal and conceal. Pratt also points out that by not changing the introduction, Burgos Debray acknowledges and takes responsibility for her controversial descriptions rather than deflecting criticism by deleting or altering her words.

6. For a detailed and insightful discussion of secrets in Menchú's discourse, see Doris Sommer's "Rigoberta's Secrets" (1991) and "No Secrets" (1996).

7. Katrak describes the tendency toward "discursive colonization" in the context of a critique of Fredric Jameson's article "World Literature in an Era of Multinational Capitalism."

8. The promotion, by Casa de las Américas, of *testimonios* over the novels of the Boom is also, as Sommer points out, a reaction against the criticism of Cuba and Castro by liberal Latin American novelists following Casto's support of the Soviet invasion of Czechoslovakia. See Sommer's *Proceed with Caution*, 117.

9. In Menchú's subsequent book, *Crossing Borders*, she describes a usual day in her life after receiving the Nobel Prize and returning to Guatemala after the signing of the peace accords. The scene she depicts includes a description of her son playing around her desk, which holds her computer. This is indeed a contrast to Menchú's depiction of the typewriter in *I, Rigoberta Menchú*. It demonstrates that human experience is not static.

10. For a more complete discussion on the potential for scholarship and pedagogy in the field to effect direct political changes, see John Beverley's article, "Can Hispanism Be a Radical Practice?"

Chapter 4. Spic Spanglish? The Reception of *Borderlands/La Frontera* and Linguistic Resistance

The word *spic* is used strategically here with full awareness of its wounding effects. It is intended to put into question the associations between discursive practices and oppression. It is also a play on the word *speak*.

1. Juan Flores and George Yúdice quote U.S. census figures in their article "Living Borders/Buscando América." The figure reflects continuous immigration over the past thirty years as well as the historical back-and-forth migration of Mexican Americans and Puerto Ricans. The term *Latino*, as used here and in census reporting, it must be noted, is heterogenous in terms of class, race, and nationality. Yet, even using the term as the umbrella label for many distinct groups, Latinos differ from other ethnic groups, such as Irish Americans or Italian Americans, in that they represent a "conquered" minority, as in the case of Chicanos and Puerto Ricans. Other Latin American migrations are fueled by economic as well as political motivations, many of which are a direct result of U.S. interventions in the region.

2. Other Chicana writers such as Cherríe Moraga and Pat Mora also interweave genres in a single text. See, for example, Moraga's *Loving in the War Years* and Pat Mora's *Nepantla*.

3. The English only movement has been chronicled and documented in detail by James Crawford. See his informative book, *Hold Your Tongue.*

4. See Rosaura Sánchez's study, *Chicano Discourse,* Ramón Saldívar's *Chicano Narrative,* and Juan Bruce-Novoa's *Retrospace: Collected Essays on Chicano Literature.*

5. José David Saldívar's book *Border Matters* reinforces the conceptualization of the United States as a map that is all border.

6. José David Saldívar's book *The Dialectics of Our America* includes chapters on Rolando Hinojosa Smith and Ntozake Shange, as writers of "our America," although they are both U.S. authors. He approaches the work of these authors through the legacy of both Martí and Retamar and argues for Casa de las Americas (which has awarded prizes to both Shange and Hinojosa) as a unifying force among the disparate parts of "our America."

7. For a discussion of Vasconcelos in the context of eugenics policies in Latin America, see Nancy Stepan's *"The Hour of Eugenics": Race, Gender and Nation in Latin America.*

8. The close ties between multiply embodied subjectivity and Chicana identity and feminism are clearly seen in the highly informative and useful anthology *Infinite Divisions,* edited by Tey Diana Rebolledo and Eliana Rivero.

9. Some of the texts that Gagnier discusses in this essay as autobiographies do not fall under that genre. *The House on Mango Street,* by Sandra Cisneros, for example, is a short story cycle that is not an autobiography, or even autobiographical, unless we subscribe to the idea that all fiction is autobiographical.

10. Various critics have explored the association between feminism—as sometimes practiced by Western (white) scholars—and colonizing practices. See for example work by Chandra Talpade Mohanty, Lila Abu-Loghod, bell hooks, and Elizabeth Weed. A particularly influential essay on this topic is Mohanty's "Under Western Eyes."

11. The term *prieta* means dark, while the term *güera* denotes light skinned, or in its most literal sense, blonde. *Güera,* however, also carries class identification, particularly in Mexico, where one's skin color is closely associated with class status. For example, depending on contextual clues, such as clothing or other signs of economic differentiation, the same individual may be classified as either *prieta* or *güera.*

12. The scripting of La Malinche as traitor has taken various forms in the twentieth century. Octavio Paz in *El laberinto de la soledad* [*The Labyrinth of Solitude*] depicts her as the double of the Virgin in the Virgin/Whore dichotomy, and as a victim of rape as well as the mother of the Mexican people. Carlos Fuentes in *Todos los gatos son pardos* scripts her as vengeful of her people and a misguided fool, nonetheless a traitor. The Mexican writer and intellectual Rosario Castellanos, in her play *El eterno femenino,* portrays La Malinche as the brains behind Cortez's success in conquering Mexico. Chicana artists have been refiguring her representation by conflating her image with that of Guadalupe. For a discussion of visions and revisions of La Malinche and Guadalupe, see Alarcón's "Traddutora, Traditora."

13. For a full and straightforward explanation of figures such as La Llorona, Malinche, and others, see Tey Diana Rebolledo's book *Women Singing in the Snow.*

14. For a contextualized discussion of the construction of the female body and female sexuality as a site of treason, see Cherríe Moraga's "A Long Line of Vendidas" in *Loving in the War Years.*

15. For fuller discussions on the position of the lesbian in Chicano culture and community, see Ellen M. Gil-Gomez's *Performing La Mestiza: Textual Representations of Lesbians of Color and the Negotiation of Identities,* and Carla Trujillo's "Chicana Lesbians: Fear and Loathing in the Chicano Community."

16. The term *invertida* as a slang term for lesbian (and *invertido* as a slang term for a male homosexual) derives from nineteenth-century pseudoscientific pamphlets and studies that pathologized homosexuality as disease. For a fuller explanation and analysis of this, see Oscar Montero's article "Julián del Casal and the Queers of Havana" and Judith Raiskin's article "Inverts and Hybrids: Lesbian Rewritings of Sexual and Racial Identities."

17. For a fuller discussion of nineteenth-century scientific discourses on race, gender, and sexuality see Sander Gilman's "Black Bodies, White Bodies: Toward an Iconography of Female Sexuality in Late Nineteenth-Century Art, Medicine and Literature," as well as "Sexology, Psychoanalysis, and Degeneration: Theory of Race to a Race to Theory" by the same author.

18. José David Saldívar, as well as other critics, has denounced *Hunger of Memory* as a conservative narrative promoting assimilation. See his article, "The School of Caliban: Pan-American Autobiography." As an example of a "gentler" or more nuanced reading of Rodríguez's text, see Barbara Frey Waxman's "Feeding the 'Hunger of Memory' and an Appetite for the Future."

19. For a similar argument, see Chela Sandoval's "U.S. Third World Feminism: The Theory and Method of Oppositional Consciousness in the Postmodern World."

Chapter 5. Coming of Age in the Curriculum: *The House on Mango Street* and *Bless Me, Ultima* as Representative Texts

1. For a fuller discussion of minorities and minority studies in institutions of higher learning, see Rosaura Sánchez's article "Ethnicity, Ideology and Academia."

2. There has been an equally if not more vocal response to this backlash, yet most of these responses have been published within the traditional channels of scholarship. See, for example, Mary Louise Pratt, "Humanities for the Future: Reflections on the Western Culture Debate at Stanford," John Guillory, "Canon, Syllabus, List," Michael Geyer, "Multiculturalism and the Politics of General Education," and Henry Louis Gates Jr., *Loose Canons.* A specific response to Hirsch's *Cultural Literacy* and Bloom's *The Closing of the American Mind* is Graywolf Press's *Multicultural Literacy: Opening the American Mind.*

3. A succinct example of the backlash's anxiety regarding the dangers of

multiculturalism is Kimball's summation of the implications of multiculturalism as an attack on what Matthew Arnold described as our common legacy, descending largely from the Greeks and the Bible which "preserves us from chaos and barbarism."

4. Anaya's novel is also frequently included in Native American Literature courses, and Cisneros's book is also frequently used in Women's Literature syllabi.

5. Chicano critic Héctor Calderón argues that, given the fact that most Chicano writers work from within educational institutions, we cannot deny "how institutionally Western our literature is." Yet, he points out, this does not erase or neutralize their cultural productions' oppositional potential.

6. For a fuller understanding and explanation of speech act theory see J. L. Austin and Paul Grice. For an explanation and discussion of reader response see Stanley Fish. Mary Louise Pratt's article, "Interpretive Strategies/Strategic Interpretations: On Anglo-American Reader Response Criticism," also offers a solid summary as well as a critique of reader response theory.

7. The term *reading competence,* as it is used here, is taken from Jonathan Culler's article "Prolegomena to a Theory of Reading" (1980).

8. Jeffrey L. Sammons, in his essay, "The Bildungsroman for Nonspecialists: An Attempt at Clarification," argues the genre's Germanness and points out misappropriations of the term in English Studies, including the work of Jerome Buckley.

9. The term *Latino* is more accepted as a blanket term, if we must have one, since it implies a strategic political alliance. For a fuller discussion of the problematic nature of labels and labeling terms as well as their history, see Suzanne Oboler's *Ethnic Labels, Latino Lives.*

10. Carlos Muñoz Jr., in his study *Youth, Identity, Power,* has argued that the term *Hispanic* in the mid-1970s became associated with a "politics on white ethnic identity" by emphasizing "whiteness" through European descent (Spain) and erasing racial and interracial identities (African, Asian, indigenous) in the Americas, specifically denying Mexican American/Chicano ties to Mexico.

11. Since the publication of Dasenbrock's article, the *PMLA* has published two other articles on Latina/o texts: one on Richard Rodríguez's *Hunger for Memory,* and another on Piri Tomás's *Down These Mean Streets.*

12. Caldrón describes the short story cycle as "prenovelistic" in that it bears parallels to Cervantes's work during the late sixteenth and early seventeenth centuries in terms of societal forces influencing production as well as audience. He argues that the form is a critique of the novel by its return to alternative structures used and developed prior to the novel's becoming "the bourgeois literary monument it is today" (Calderón 100).

13. For contextualized readings of *The House on Mango Street* in relation to a Chicano formative tradition in the short story cycle, see Erlinda González-Berry and Tey Diana Rebolledo's article "Growing up Chicano: Tomás Rivera and Sandra Cisneros" and Renato Rosaldo's "Fables of the Fallen Guy."

Conclusion: Coyotes in the Classroom

1. The essay that describes the teaching of Menchú's *testimonio* in relation to the slave narrative is "Rigoberta Menchú's Testimony as Required First Year Reading" by Jonnie G. Guerra and Sharon Ahern Fechter. Another similarity the essay explores is that of the role of literacy, as well as the gender issues raised by both Menchú's story and Harriet Ann Jacobs's narrative of her life in *Incidents in the Life of a Slave Girl.*

2. Not surprisingly, the text traditionally thought to mark the beginning of *testimonio* as a recognized genre, *Biografía de un cimarrón* [*The Autobiography of a Runaway Slave*], can be classified as both a *testimonio* and a slave narrative of sorts.

3. See Stephen Benz's article "Culture Shock and *I, Rigoberta Menchú*" and suggested teaching materials included in the appendix to *Teaching and Testimony.*

4. The course that José David Saldívar describes was titled "American Lives" and was designed and taught by Chicano writer and intellectual Arturo Islas.

Bibliography

Abel, Elizabeth, Marianne Hirsch, and Elizabeth Langland, eds. *The Voyage In: Fictions of Female Development.* Hanover, N.H.: University Press of New England, 1983. 1–27.

Abu-Lughod, Lila. "Can There Be a Feminist Ethnography?" *Women and Performance* 5.1 (1990): 7–27.

Alarcón, Norma. "Chicana Feminism: In the Tracks of 'The' Native Woman." *Cultural Studies* 4.3 (1990): 248–63.

———. "Traddutora, Traditora: A Paradigmatic Figure of Chicana Feminism." *Cultural Critique* 13 (1990): 57–87.

Anaya, Rudolfo. *Bless Me, Ultima.* Berkeley: Tonatiuh, 1972.

Anzaldúa, Gloria. *Borderlands/La Frontera: The New Mestiza.* San Francisco: Spinster/Aunt Lute, 1987.

Arenas, Reinaldo. *Before Night Falls.* Trans. Dolores M. Koch. New York: Viking, 1993.

Arias, Arturo. "Authoring Ethnicized Subjects: Rigoberta Menchú and the Performative Production of the Subaltern Self." *PMLA* 116.1 (2001): 75–88.

Arnold, Matthew. "The Function of Criticism at the Present Time." *The Portable Matthew Arnold.* Ed. Lionel Trilling. New York: Viking, 1949. 234–266.

Arteaga, Alfred. "An Other Tongue." *An Other Tongue: Nation and Ethnicity in the Linguistic Borderlands.* Ed. Alfred Arteaga. Durham: Duke University Press, 1994. 9–33.

Austin, J. L. *How to Do Things with Words.* New York: Oxford University Press, 1965.

Baker, Houston. "Caliban's Triple Play." *"Race," Writing and Difference.* Ed. Henry Louis Gates Jr. Chicago: University of Chicago Press, 1995. 381–95.

Bakhtin, Mikhail M. *The Dialogic Imagination.* Ed. M. Holquist. Trans. Caryl Emerson and Michael Holquist. Austin: University of Texas Press, 1981.

Barnet, Miguel. *Biografía de un cimarrón* [*Autobiography of a Runaway Slave*]. Barcelona: Ediciones Ariel, 1994.

Bartra, Roger. *The Cage of Melancholy: Identity and Metamorphosis in the Mexi-*

can Character. Trans. Christopher Hall. New Brunswick, N.J.: Rutgers University Press, 1992.

Behar, Ruth. *Translated Woman: Crossing the Border with Esperanza's Story.* Boston: Beacon, 1993.

———. *The Vulnerable Observer: Anthropology that Breaks Your Heart.* Boston: Beacon, 1996.

Bell, Steven M. "A Prolegomenon." *Critical Theory, Cultural Politics, and Latin American Narrative.* Ed. Steven M. Bell, Albert H. LeMay, and Leonard Orr. Notre Dame: University of Notre Dame Press, 1993. 1–32.

Benjamin, Walter. "The Task of the Translator." *Delos: A Journal on and of Translation* 2 (1968): 76–99.

Benz, Stephen. "Culture Shock and *I, Rigoberta Menchú.*" *Teaching and Testimony: Rigoberta Menchú and the North American Classroom.* Ed. Stephen Benz and Allen Carey-Webb. Albany: State University of New York Press, 1996. 19–26.

Beverley, John. "Can Hispanism Be a Radical Practice?" *Ideologies and Literature: Journal of Hispanic and Lusophone Discourse Analysis* 4.16 (1983): 9–22.

———. "The Margin at the Center: On Testimonio." *Modern Fiction Studies* 35.1 (1989): 11–28.

———. "The Real Thing." *The Real Thing: Testimonial Discourse and Latin America.* Ed. George M. Gugelberger. Durham: Duke University Press, 1996. 266–86.

———. *Subalternity and Representation: Arguments in Cultural Theory.* Durham: Duke University Press, 1999.

———. "'Through All Things Modern': Second Thoughts on Testimonio." *Boundary 2* 18.2 (1991): 1–21.

Bhabha, Homi K. "The World and the Home." *Social Text* 10.2–3 (1992): 141–53.

Bloom, Allan. *The Closing of the American Mind.* New York: Simon and Schuster, 1987.

Borges, Jorge Luis. "Pierre Menard, autor del Quijote." *Ficciones.* Buenos Aires: Emece Editores, 1956.

Bruce-Novoa, Juan. "Canonical and Non-canonical Texts." *The Americas Review.* 14.3–4 (1996): 119–35.

———. *Retrospace: Collected Essays on Chicano Literature.* Houston: Arte Público, 1990.

Brushwood, John S. "Two Views of the Boom: North and South." *Latin American Literary Review.* 15.29 (1987): 13–23.

Burgos Debray, Elisabeth. *Me llamo Rigoberta Menchú y así me nació la conciencia.* Barcelona: Argos Vergara, 1983.

Calderón, Héctor. "The Novel and the Community of Readers: Reading Tomás Rivera's *Y no se lo tragó la tierra.*" *Criticism in the Borderlands: Studies in Chicano Literature, Culture, and Ideology.* Ed. Héctor Calderón and José David Saldívar. Durham: Duke University Press, 1991. 97–113.

Califa, Antonio J. "Declaring English the Official Language: Prejudice Spoken Here." *Harvard Civil Rights-Civil Liberties Law Review* 24 (1989): 320–34.

Canclini, Néstor García. *Culturas Hibridas* [*Hybrid Cultures*]. Mexico City: Grijalbo-Conaculta, 1989.

Carpentier, Alejo. "De lo real maravilloso americano." *Tientos, diferencias y otros ensayos.* Barcelona: Plaza y Janes Editores, 1987.

———. "On the Marvelous Real in America." Trans. Tanya Huntington and Lois Parkinson Zamora. *Magical Realism: Theory, History, Community.* Ed. Lois Parkinson Zamora and Wendy B. Faris. Durham: Duke University Press, 1995. 76–88.

Carr, Robert. "Re-presentando el testimonio: notas sobre el cruce divisorio primer mundo/tercer mundo." *Revista crítica literaria* 18.36 (1992): 73–94.

Castellanos, Rosario. *El eterno femenino: farsa.* Mexico: Fondo de Cultura Económica, 1975.

Chabram-Dernersesian, Angie. "I Throw Punches for My Race, but I Don't Want to Be a Man: Writing Us—Chica-nos (Girl,Us)/Chicanas—into the Movement Script." *Cultural Studies.* Ed. Lawrence Grossberg, Cary Nelson, and Paula Treichler. New York: Routledge, 1992. 81–95.

Chauncey, George. "From Sexual Inversion to Homosexuality." *Salmagundi* 58–59 (1982–83): 114–46.

Christian, Karen. "Performing Magical Realism: The 'Boom' in U.S. Latino Literature." *The Americas Review* 24.3–4 (1996): 166–78.

Cisneros, Sandra. *The House on Mango Street.* Houston: Arte Público, 1986.

———. "Salvador Late or Early." *Iguana Dreams: New Latino Fiction.* Ed. Delia Poey and Virgil Suarez. New York: HarperCollins, 1992.

Clifford, James. *The Predicament of Culture: Twentieth Century Ethnography, Literature, and Art.* Cambridge: Harvard University Press, 1988.

Codrescu, Andrei. "*Raining Backwards* (Review)." *The New York Times Book Review,* 14 Aug. 1988: 27.

Cofer, Judith Ortiz. *The Line of the Sun.* Athens: University of Georgia Press, 1989.

Colás, Santiago. *Postmodernity in Latin America: The Argentine Paradigm.* Durham: Duke University Press, 1994.

Collazo, Oscar. *Literatura en la revolución y revolución en la literatura.* Montevideo: Marcha, 1969.

Crawford, James. *Hold Your Tongue: Bilingualism and the Politics of "English Only."* Reading, Mass.: Addison Wesley, 1992.

Culler, Jonathan. "Prolegomena to a Theory of Reading." *The Reader in the Text: Essays on Audience and Interpretations.* Ed. Susan R. Suliman and Inge Crosman. Princeton: Princeton University Press, 1980. 46–66.

Dasenbrock, Reed Way. "Intelligibility and Meaningfulness in Multicultural Literature in English." *PMLA* 102.1 (1987): 10–19.

Davies, Carole Boyce. "Collaboration and the Ordering Imperative in Life Story Production." *De/Colonizing the Subject: The Politics of Gender in Women's*

Autobiography. Ed. Sidonie Smith and Julia Watson. Minneapolis: University of Minnesota Press, 1992. 3–19.

Dávila, Alberto, Alok K. Bahara, and Rogelio Saenz. "Accent Penalties and the Earnings of Mexican Americans." *Social Science Quarterly* 77.4 (1993): 902–17.

Derrida, Jacques. "The Law of Genre." Trans. Avital Ronell. *Glyph* 7 (1980): 203–4.

———. "Plato's Pharmacy." *Dissemination.* Trans. Barbara Johnson. Chicago: University of Chicago Press, 1981. 63–119.

Dillard, Annie. *An American Childhood.* New York: Harper and Row, 1987.

Doctorow, E. L. "False Documents." *American Review* 26 (1977): 231.

Donoso, José. *The Boom in Spanish American Literature, A Personal History.* Trans. Gregory Kolovakos. New York: Columbia University Press, 1977.

Duncan, J. Ann. *Voices, Visions and a New Reality.* Pittsburgh: University of Pittsburgh Press, 1986.

Durix, Jean-Pierre. "Magical Realism in *Midnight's Children.*" *Commonwealth* 8.1 (1985): 57–63.

Earle, Peter. "Back to the Center: Hispanic American Fiction Today." *Hispanic Review* 58.1 (1990): 19–35.

Echevarría, Roberto González. *Myth and Archive: A Theory of Latin American Narrative.* Cambridge: Cambridge University Press, 1990.

Fernández, Roberto. *Holy Radishes!* Houston: Arte Público, 1995.

———. *Raining Backwards.* Houston: Arte Público, 1988.

Ferré, Rosario. "El coloquio de las perras." *Quimera: Revista de literatura* 130 (1994): 26–39.

Fish, Stanley. *Is There a Text in This Class?* Cambridge: Harvard University Press, 1980.

Flores, Angel. "Magical Realism in Spanish American Fiction." *Magical Realism: Theory, History, Community.* Ed. Lois Parkinson Zamora and Wendy B. Faris. Durham: Duke University Press, 1995. 109–17.

Flores, Juan, and George Yúdice. "Living Borders/Buscando América: Languages of Latino Self-Formation." *Social Text* 24 (1990): 57–84.

Foster, David William. *Alternate Voices in the Contemporary Latin American Narrative.* Columbia: Missouri University Press, 1985.

Franco, Jean. "Beyond Ethnocentrism: Gender, Power, and the Third-World Intelligentsia." *Marxism and the Interpretation of Culture.* Ed. Lawrence Grossberg and Cary Nelson. Urbana: University of Illinois Press, 1988. 503–15.

———. *Plotting Women: Gender and Representation in Mexico.* New York: Columbia University Press, 1989.

Frank, Gayla. "Ruth Behar's Biography in the Shadow: A Review of Reviews." *American Anthropologist* 97.2 (1995): 357–59.

Friedman, Susan Stanford. "Women's Autobiographical Selves: Theory and Practice." *The Primitive Self: Theory and Practice of Women's Autobiography.* Ed. Shari Benstock. Chapel Hill: University of North Carolina Press, 1988. 34–62.

Fuentes, Carlos. *Todos los gatos son pardos.* Mexico: Siglo Veintiuno, 1977.

Fusco, Coco. "Passionate Irreverence: The Cultural Politics of Identity." *English Is Broken Here, Notes on Cultural Fusion in the Americas.* New York: The New Press, 1995. 23–36.

Gagnier, Regenia. "Feminist Autobiography in the 1980s." *Feminist Studies* 17.1 (1991): 135–48.

Galeano, Eduardo. "Porfiada fe." *Casa de las Américas* 174 (1989): 126–27.

Gass, William H. "The First Seven Pages of the Boom." *Latin American Literary Review* 15.29 (1987): 33–39.

Gates, Henry Louis Jr. *Loose Canons: Notes on the Culture Wars.* Oxford: Oxford University Press, 1992.

Geisdorfer Feal, Rosemary. "Spanish Autobiography and the Slave Narrative Tradition: *Biografía de un cimarrón* and *Me llamo Rigoberta Menchú.*" *Modern Language Studies* 20.1 (1990): 100–111.

Geyer, Michael. "Multiculturalism and the Politics of General Education." *Critical Inquiry* (1993): 499–533.

Gil-Gomez, Ellen M. *Performing La Mestiza: Textual Representations of Lesbians of Color and the Negotiation of Identities.* New York: Garland, 2000.

Gilman, Sander L. "Black Bodies, White Bodies: Toward an Iconography of Female Sexuality in Late Nineteenth-Century Art, Medicine and Literature." *Critical Inquiry* 12.1 (1985): 204–42.

———. "Sexology, Psychoanalysis, and Degeneration: Theory of Race to a Race to Theory." *Degeneration: The Dark Side of Progress.* Ed. J. Edward Chamberlin and Sander L. Gilman. New York: Columbia University Press, 1985. 72–96.

Goldberg, David Theo. "Multicultural Conditions." *Multiculturalism: A Critical Reader.* Ed. David Theo Goldberg. Cambridge: Blackwell, 1994. 1–44.

Gómez-Peña, Guillermo. *Warrior for Gringostroika.* Saint Paul, Minn.: Graywolf, 1993.

González, Aníbal. "Translation and Genealogy: *One Hundred Years of Solitude.*" *Gabriel García Márquez: New Readings.* Ed. Bernard McGuirk and Richard Cardwell. Cambridge: Cambridge University Press, 1987. 65–80.

González-Berry, Erlinda, and Tey Diana Rebolledo. "Growing up Chicano: Tomás Rivera and Sandra Cisneros." *International Studies in Honor of Tomás Rivera.* Ed. Julian Olivåres. Houston: Arte Público, 1986. 109–20.

Grice, Paul. "Logic and Conversation." *Speech Acts: Syntax and Semantics.* Ed. Peter Cole and Jerry L. Morgan. New York: Academic, 1975. 41–58.

Guenther, Irene. "Magic Realism, New Objectivity, and the Arts During the Weimar Republic." *Magical Realism: Theory, History, Community.* Ed. Lois Parkinson Zamora and Wendy B. Farris. Durham: Duke University Press, 1995. 33–73.

Guerra, Jonnie G., and Sharon Ahern Fechter. "Rigoberta Menchú's Testimony as Required First Year Reading." *Teaching and Testimony: Rigoberta Menchú and the North American Classroom.* Ed. Stephen Benz and Allen Carey-Webb. Albany: State University of New York Press, 1996. 261–70.

Guillory, John. "Canon, Syllabus, List: A Note on the Pedagogic Imaginary." *Transition* 52 (1991): 36–54.

Gunn, Janet Verner. "A Window of Opportunity: An Ethics of Reading Third-World Autobiography." *Teaching and Testimony: Rigoberta Menchú and the North American Classroom.* Ed. Stephen Benz and Allen Carey-Webb. Albany: State University of New York Press, 1996. 271–78.

Gusdorf, Georges. "Conditions and Limits of Autobiography." *Autobiography: Essays Theoretical and Critical.* Ed. James Olney. Princeton: Princeton University Press, 1980. 28–47.

Gutiérrez-Jones, Leslie. "Different Voices: The Re-Bildung of the Barrio in Sandra Cisneros' *The House on Mango Street.*" *Anxious Power: Reading, Writing and Ambivalence in Narrative by Women.* Ed. Carol J. Singley and Susan Elizabeth Sweeney. Albany: State University of New York Press, 1993. 295–312.

Haraway, Donna. *Simians, Cyborgs, and Women: The Reinvention of Women.* New York: Routledge, 1991.

Harlow, Barbara. "All That Is Inside Is Not Center." *Coming to Terms: Feminism, Theory, Politics.* Ed. Elizabeth Weed. New York: Routledge, 1989.

———. *Resistance Literature.* New York: Methuen, 1987.

Hartstock, Nancy. "Foucault on Power: A Theory for Women?" *Feminism/Postmodernism.* Ed. Linda J. Nicholson. New York: Routledge, 1990. 157–75.

Herrero-Olaizola, Alejandro. "Consuming Aesthetics: Seix Barral and José Donoso in the Field of Latin American Literary Production." *Modern Language Notes* 115.2 (2000): 323–29.

Hicks, Emily D. *Border Writing: The Multidimensional Text.* Minneapolis: University of Minnesota Press, 1991.

Hirsch, E. D. Jr. *Cultural Literacy: What Every American Needs to Know.* Boston: Houghton Mifflin, 1987.

hooks, bell. *Teaching to Transgress: Education as the Practice of Freedom.* New York: Routledge, 1994.

Jacobs, Harriet A. *Incidents in the Life of a Slave Girl.* Ed. Jean Fagan Yellin. Cambridge: Harvard University Press, 1987.

Jameson, Fredric. "De la situación de importaciónes literarias y culturales en el tercer mundo: El caso de testimonio." *Revista de crítica literaria* 18.36 (1992): 117–33.

———. "World Literature in an Age of Multinational Capitalism." *The Current in Criticism: Essays on the Present and Future in Literary Theory.* Ed. Clayton Koelb and Virgil Lokke. West Lafayette: Purdue University Press, 1987. 139–158.

JanMohamed, Abdul. "Worldliness-without-World, Homelessness-as-Home: Toward a Definition of the Specular Border Intellectual." *Edward Said: A Critical Reader.* Ed. Michael Sprinker. Oxford: Blackwell, 1992. 96–120.

Johnson, David E., and Scott Michaelsen. Introduction. *Border Theory: The Limits of Cultural Politics.* Ed. David E. Johnson and Scott Michaelsen. Minneapolis: University of Minnesota Press, 1991.

Kaplan, Caren. "Resisting Autobiography: Out-Law Genres and Transnational Feminist Subjects." *De/Colonizing the Subject: The Politics of Gender in Women's Autobiography.* Ed. Sidonie Smith and Julia Watson. Minneapolis: University of Minnesota Press, 1992. 115–32.

Katrak, Ketu H. "Decolonizing Culture: Toward a Theory for Postcolonial Women's Texts." *Modern Fiction Studies* 35.1 (1989): 157–79.

Kimball, Roger. *Tenured Radicals: How Politics Has Corrupted Higher Education.* New York: Harper Collins, 1990.

Kingsolver, Barbara. "Desert Heat." *Los Angeles Times Book Review,* 16 May 1993: 1.

Klinkowitz, Jerome. *The Self-Apparent Word: Fiction as Language/Language as Fiction.* Carbondale: Southern Illinois University Press, 1984.

Labovitz, Esther Kleinbord. *The Myth of the Heroine: The Female Bidungsroman in the Twentieth Century.* New York: Peter Lang, 1986.

Larson, Neil. Foreword. *Border Writing: The Multidimensional Text,* by Emily Hicks. Minneapolis: University of Minnesota Press, 1991.

Limón, José. *Dancing with the Devil: Society and Cultural Poetics in Mexican-American South Texas.* Madison: University of Wisconsin Press, 1994.

Lindstrom, Naomi. *Twentieth-Century Spanish American Fiction.* Austin: University of Texas Press, 1994.

Marcos, Juan Manuel. *De García Márquez al Post-Boom.* Madrid: Orígenes, 1986.

Márquez, Gabriel García. *One Hundred Years of Solitude.* Trans. Gregory Rabassa. New York: Avon, 1971.

Martí, José. *Obras Completas.* Vol. 4. Havana: Editorial Nacional de Cuba, 1966.

Martin, Gerald. *Journeys through the Labyrinth: Latin American Fiction in the Twentieth Century.* New York: Verso, 1989.

McLaren, Peter. "White Terror and Oppositional Agency: Toward a Critical Multiculturalism." *Multiculturalism: A Critical Reader.* Ed. David Theo Goldberg. Cambridge: Blackwell, 1994. 45–74.

Meese, Elizabeth. "(Dis)locations: Reading the Theory of a Third World Woman in *I . . . Rigoberta Menchú.*" *(Ex)tensions: Re- Figuring Feminist Criticism.* Urbana: University of Illinois Press, 1990. 97–128.

Menchú, Rigoberta. *Crossing Borders.* Trans. Ann Wright. London: Verso, 1998.

———. *I, Rigoberta Menchú: An Indian Women in Guatemala.* Ed. Elisabeth Burgos Debray. Trans. Ann White. London: Verso, 1984.

Mignolo, Walter. "Canons A(nd) Cross-Cultural Boundaries (or, Whose Canon Are We Talking About?)" *Poetics Today* 2.1 (1991): 1–28.

Miller, Christopher. *Blank Darkness: Africanist Discourse in French.* Chicago: University of Chicago Press, 1989.

Mohan, Rajeswari. "Dodging the Crossfire: Questions for Postcolonial Pedagogy." *Order and Partialities: Theory, Pedagogy and the "Postcolonial."* Ed. Myrsiades Kostas and Jerry McGuire. Albany: State University of New York Press, 1995. 361–84.

Mohanty, Chandra Talpade. "Under Western Eyes: Feminist Scholarship and Colonial Discourse." *Boundary 2* 22.3 (1984): 3–13.

Monegal, Emil Rodríguez. *El boom de la novela latinoamericana.* Caracas: Editorial Tiempo Nuevo, 1972.

Montero, Oscar. "Julián del Casal and the Queers of Havana." *¿Entiendes? Queer Readings, Hispanic Writings.* Ed. Emilie Bergman and Paul Julia Smith. Durham: Duke University Press, 1995. 92–112.

Mora, Pat. *Nepantla.* Albuquerque: University of New Mexico Press, 1993.

Moraga, Cherríe. *Loving in the War Years/Lo que nunca pasó por sus labios.* Boston: South End, 1983.

Morgan, Speer, et al. "Publication Is Not Recommended: From the Knopf Files." *The Missouri Review* 23.3 (2000): 83–186.

Muñoz, Carlos Jr. *Youth, Identity, Power.* London: Verso, 1989.

Oboler, Suzanne. *Ethnic Labels, Latino Lives: Identity and the Politics of (Re)Presentation in the United States.* Minneapolis: University of Minnesota Press, 1995.

Ong, Walter J. *Orality and Literacy: The Technologizing of the Word.* New York: Methuen, 1982.

Patai, Daphne. "Sick and Tired of Scholars' Nouveau Solipsism." *The Chronicle of Higher Education,* 23 Feb. 1994. A52.

Paz, Octavio. *The Labyrinth of Solitude.* Trans. Lysander Kemp. New York: Grove, 1961.

Peden, Margaret Sayers. "Translating the Boom: The Apple Theory of Translation." *Latin American Literary Review* 15.29 (1987): 159–72.

Pérez, Emma. "Irigaray's Female Symbolic in the Making of Chicana Lesbian *Sitios y Lenguas* (Sites and Discourses)." *The Lesbian Postmodern.* Ed. Laura Doan. New York: Columbia University Press, 1994. 104–7.

Phelan, Shane. "Coyote Politics: Trickster Tales and Feminist Futures." *Hypatia* 11.3 (1996): 130–49.

Planellas, Antonio. "La polémica sobre el realismo mágico en Hispanoamérica." *Revista inter-americana de bibliografía/Inter-American Review of Bibliography* 37 (1987): 517–29.

Pratt, Anais. *Archetypal Patterns in Women's Fiction.* Bloomington: Indiana University Press, 1981.

Pratt, Mary Louise. "Criticism in the Contact Zone: Decentering Community and Nation." *Critical Theory, Cultural Politics, and Latin American Narrative.* Ed. Steven M. Bell, Albert H. Le May, and Leonard Orr. Notre Dame: University of Notre Dame Press, 1993. 83–102.

———. "Humanities for the Future: Reflections on the Western Culture Debate at Stanford." *South Atlantic Quarterly* 89.1 (1990): 7–25.

———. "Interpretive Strategies/Strategic Interpretations: On Anglo-American Reader Response Criticism." *Boundary 2* 11.1–2 (1982): 201–31.

Rabassa, Gregory. "No Two Snowflakes Are Alike: Translation as Metaphor." *The*

Craft of Translation. Ed. John Biguenet and Rainer Schulte. Chicago: University of Chicago Press, 1989. 1–12.

Rabinowitz, Paula. "Naming, Magic, and Documentary: The Subversion of the Narrative in *Song of Solomon, Ceremony,* and *China Men.*" *Feminist Revisions: What Has Been and What Might Be.* Ed. Vivian Patrake and Louise Tilly. Ann Arbor: University of Michigan Press, 1983. 26–42.

Raiskin, Judith. "Inverts and Hybrids: Lesbian Rewritings of Sexual and Racial Identities." *The Lesbian Postmodern.* Ed. Laura Doan. New York: Columbia University Press, 1994. 156–72.

Rama, Angel. "El Boom en perspectiva." *Más allá del Boom.* Ed. David Viñas. Buenos Aires: Folios, 1984.

———. *La ciudad letrada* [*The Lettered City*]. Hanover, N.H.: Ediciones del Norte, 1984.

Rebolledo, Tey Diana. *Women Singing in the Snow: A Cultural Analysis of Chicana Literature.* Tucson: University of Arizona Press, 1995.

Rebolledo, Tey Diana, and Eliana S. Rivero, eds. *Infinite Divisions: An Anthology of Chicana Literature.* Tucson: University of Arizona Press, 1993.

Rechy, John. *The Miraculous Day of Amelia Gómez.* New York: Arcade/Little Brown, 1991.

Retamar, Roberto Fernández. *Caliban and Other Essays.* Trans. Edward Baker. Minneapolis: University of Minnesota Press, 1989.

Rincón, Carlos. "Modernidad periférica y el dasafío de lo postmoderno: perspectivas del arte narrativo latinoamericano." *Revista de Crítica Literaria Latinoamericana* 15.25 (1989): 16–24.

Ríos, Alberto Alvaro. *Pig Cookies and Other Stories.* San Francisco: Chronicle Books, 1995.

Rivera, Tomás. *. . . y no se lo tragó la tierra.* Berkeley: Quinto Sol, 1971.

Rodríguez, Richard. *Hunger of Memory: The Education of Richard Rodríguez.* Boston: D. R. Godine, 1981.

Rosaldo, Renato. *Culture and Truth: The Remaking of Social Analysis.* Boston: Beacon, 1989.

———. "Fables of the Fallen Guy." *Criticism in the Borderlands: Studies in Chicano Literature, Culture, and Ideology.* Ed. Héctor Calderón and José David Saldívar. Durham: Duke University Press, 1991. 84–93.

Rumold, Inca. "Independencia cultural de Latinoamérica." *Plural* 241 (1991): 21.

Said, Edward. *Orientalism.* New York: Pantheon, 1978.

Saldívar, José David. *Border Matters: Remapping American Cultural Studies.* Berkeley: University of California Press, 1997.

———. *The Dialectics of Our America.* Durham: Duke University Press, 1987.

———. "The School of Caliban: Pan-American Autobiography." *Multicultural Autobiography: American Lives.* Ed. James Robert Payne. Knoxville: University of Tennessee Press, 1992. 297–325.

Saldívar, Ramón. *Chicano Narrative: The Dialectics of Difference.* Madison: University of Wisconsin Press, 1990.

Saldívar-Hull, Sonia. *Feminism on the Border: Chicana Gender Politics and Literature.* Berkeley: University of California Press, 2000.

Sammons, Jeffrey L. "The Bildungsroman for Nonspecialists: An Attempt at a Clarification." *Reflection and Action: Essays on the Bildungsroman.* Ed. James Hardin. Columbia: University of South Carolina Press, 1991. 26–45.

Sánchez, Alejandro. "Alejandro Sánchez." *The Americas Review.* 23.1–2 (1995): 30–41.

Sánchez, Rosaura. *Chicano Discourse: Socio-Historic Perspectives* (1983). Houston: Arte Público, 1994.

———. "Ethnicity, Ideology and Academia." *The Americas Review* 15.1 (1987): 80–88.

Sandoval, Chela. "Feminism and Racism: A Report on the 1981 National Women's Studies Conference." *Making Face, Making Soul/ Haciendo Caras: Creative and Critical Perspectives by Feminists of Color.* Ed. Gloria Anzaldúa. San Francisco: Spinster/Aunt Lute, 1990. 55–71.

———. "U.S. Third World Feminism: The Theory and Method of Oppositional Consciousness in the Postmodern World." *Genders* 10 (1991): 1–24.

Santana, Mario. *Foreigners in the Homeland: The Spanish American Novel in Spain, 1962–1974.* Lewisburg, Penn.: Bucknell University Press, 2000.

Schaffer, Randolph P. *The Apprenticeship Novel: A Study of the "Bildungsroman" as a Regulative Type in Western Literature with a Focus on Three Classic Representatives by Goethe, Maugham, and Mann.* New York: Peter Lang, 1984.

Scheel, Charles. "Les romans de Jean-Louis Bahio'o et le réalisme merveilleux redéfini." *Présence Africaine: Revue Culturalle du Monde Noir* 147.3 (1988): 43–62.

Sedgwick, Eve Kosofsky. *Tendencies.* Durham: Duke University Press, 1993.

Shaw, Donald L. "Concerning the Interpretation of *Cien años de soledad.*" *Ibero-Amerikanisches Archiv* 3 (1977): 318–29.

———. *Nueva narrativa hispanoamericana,* 5th ed. Madrid: Cátedra, 1992.

Simonson, Rick, and Scott Walker, eds. *Multicultural Literacy: Opening the American Mind.* Saint Paul, Minn.: Graywolf, 1988.

Skármeta, Antonio. "La novísima generación: varias características y un límite." *Revista de Literatura Hispanoamericana* 10 (1976): 9–18.

Smith, Sidonie, and Julia Watson. Introduction. *De/colonizing the Subject: The Politics of Gender in Women's Autobiography.* Minneapolis: University of Minnesota Press, 1992.

Smorkaloff, Pamela. "De las crónicas al testimonio: sociocrítica y comunidad histórica en las letras Latinoamericanas." *Nuevo Texto Crítico* 4.8 (1991): 101–16.

Sommer, Doris. "Be-longing and Bi-lingual States." *Diacritics* 29.4 (1999): 84–115.

———. *Foundational Fictions: The National Romances of Latin America.* Berkeley: University of California Press, 1991.

———. "No Secrets." *The Real Thing: Testimonial Discourse and Latin America.* Ed. George Gugelberger. Durham: Duke University Press, 1996. 130–57.

———. *Proceed with Caution, When Engaged by Minority Writing in the Americas.* Cambridge: Harvard University Press, 1999.

———. "Rigoberta's Secrets." *Latin American Perspectives* 18.3 (1991): 25–50.

Spelman, Elizabeth V. *Inessential Woman: Problems of Exclusion in Feminist Thought.* Boston: Beacon, 1988.

Spivak, Gayatri Chakravorty. "Can the Subaltern Speak? Speculations on Widow Sacrifice." *Marxism and the Interpretation of Culture.* Ed. Lawrence Grossberg and Cary Nelson. Urbana: University of Illinois Press, 1988. 271–313.

———. *Outside in the Teaching Machine.* New York: Routledge, 1993.

Stepan, Nancy. *"The Hour of Eugenics": Race, Gender and Nation in Latin America.* Ithaca: Cornell University Press, 1990.

Stoll, David. *Rigoberta Menchú and the Story of All Poor Guatemalans.* Boulder: Westview, 1999.

Telles, Edward E. "The Continuing Significance of Phenotype Among Mexican Americans." *Social Science Quarterly* 73.1 (1992): 120–23.

Torgovnick, Marianna. *Gone Primitive: Savage Intellects, Modern Lives.* Chicago: University of Chicago Press, 1990.

Trujillo, Carla. "Chicana Lesbians: Fear and Loathing in the Chicano Community." *Chicana Lesbians: The Girls Our Mothers Warned Us About.* Ed. Carla Trujillo. Berkeley: Third Woman, 1991. 186–94.

Uttal, Lynne. "Inclusion without Influence: The Continuing Tokenism of Women of Color." *Making Face, Making Soul/Haciendo Caras: Creative and Critical Perspectives by Feminists of Color.* Ed. Gloria Anzaldúa. San Francisco: Spinster/Aunt Lute, 1990. 42–45.

Vasconcelos, José. *La raza cósmica [The Cosmic Race]* (1925). Trans. Didier Jaén. Los Angeles: California State University Press, 1979.

Vidal, Hernán. *Literatura hispanoamericana e ideología liberal: surgimento y crisis.* Buenos Aires: Hispamérica, 1976.

Villareal, José Antonio. *Pocho.* New York: Simon and Schuster, 1956.

Watson, Richard A. "A Pig's Tail." *Latin American Literary Review* 15.29 (Jan.-June, 1987): 89–92.

Waxman, Barbara Frey. "Feeding the 'Hunger of Memory' and an Appetite for the Future." *Cross-Addressing: Resistance Literature and Cultural Borders.* Ed. John C. Hawley. Albany: State University of New York Press, 1996. 207–19.

Weed, Elizabeth, ed. *Coming to Terms: Feminism, Theory, Politics.* New York: Routledge, 1989.

Williams, Raymond L. Preface. *The Boom in Retrospect. Latin American Literary Review* 15.29 (1987): 8.

Yarbro-Bejarano, Yvonne. "Gloria Anzaldúa's *Borderlands/La Frontera:* Cultural Studies, Difference, and the Non-Unitary Subject." *Cultural Critique* 28 (1994): 5–27.

Yúdice, George. "*Testimonio* and Postmodernism." *The Real Thing: Testimonial Discourse and Latin America.* Ed. George M. Gugelberger. Durham: Duke University Press, 1996. 42–57.

Zamora, Lois Parkinson, and Wendy B. Faris, eds. *Magical Realism: Theory, History, Community.* Durham: Duke University Press, 1995.

Zimmerman, Marc. "*Testimonio* in Guatemala: Payeras, Rigoberta, and Beyond." *The Real Thing: Testimonial Discourse and Latin America.* Ed. George M. Gugelberger. Durham: Duke University Press, 1996. 101–29.

Zinn, Maxine Baca, et al. "The Cost of Exclusionary Practices in Women's Studies." *Making Face, Making Soul/Haciendo Caras: Creative and Critical Perspectives by Feminists of Color.* Ed. Gloria Anzaldúa. San Francisco: Spinster/Aunt Lute, 1990. 29–41.

Zúñiga, Victor. "The Changing Face of Border Culture Studies." *NACLA Report on the Americas* 33.3 (1999): 36–39.

Index

Delia Poey is assistant professor in the Department of Modern Languages and Linguistics at Florida State University. She has coedited two anthologies, *Iguana Dreams: New Latino Fiction* and *Little Havana Blues: A Cuban-American Literature Anthology,* as well as edited *Out of the Mirror Garden,* a collection of fiction by Latin American women.

www.ingramcontent.com/pod-product-compliance
Lightning Source LLC
LaVergne TN
LVHW051007080826
845145LV00009B/2494

* 9 7 8 1 6 1 6 1 0 1 3 1 2 *